TABLE OF CONTENTS

You will be with child and give birth to a son,
and you are to give him the name Jesus (1:31).

—— 1 ——
Preface, Jesus' Birth, and Boyhood
Luke 1:1–2:52

DIMENSION ONE:
WHAT DOES THE BIBLE SAY?

Answer these questions by reading Luke 1

1. Who is the writer who refers to himself as "me"? (1:3)

2. What is the purpose of Luke's Gospel? (1:4)

3. What does Luke say is his method of writing? (1:1-3)

4. What sources does Luke use in compiling his Gospel? (1:1-2)

5. How does Luke describe Herod, Zechariah, and Elizabeth? (1:5-7)

6. What is Zechariah doing in the Temple? (1:8)

7. How does Zechariah respond to the angel's promise of a prophetic son? (1:18, 22)

8. What words does Gabriel use to greet Mary? (1:28)

9. Over what people does Gabriel say Jesus will reign? (1:32-33)

10. What unique, divine event does Gabriel tell Mary will happen in her life? (1:35)

11. What does Mary learn about her relative Elizabeth? (1:36)

12. What names does the angel tell Zechariah and Mary to give their sons? (1:13, 31)

13. In response to Elizabeth's warm greetings, how does Mary answer? (1:46-47)

14. After staying three months with Elizabeth, where does Mary go? (1:56)

15. How does Zechariah confirm the naming of his son? (1:63)

16. One of Luke's special interests is the Holy Spirit. What does he say about the Holy Spirit and Mary, Elizabeth, and Zechariah? (1:35, 41, 67)

17. About whom does Zechariah sing his praises? (1:68-79)

Answer these questions by reading Luke 2

18. Why are Joseph and Mary going to Bethlehem? (2:1-5)

19. What is the message of the heavenly host to the shepherds? (2:14)

20. What happens on the eighth day after Jesus' birth? (2:21)

21. What do Mary and Joseph offer as a sacrifice in their son's behalf? (2:22-24)

22. What do Joseph and Mary do after meeting the requirements of the law? (2:39)

23. How often do Joseph and Mary visit Jerusalem? (2:41)

24. When Jesus is twelve, what is he doing at the Temple, after the Feast of the Passover? (2:42-49)

25. How does Luke describe Jesus' growth and development? (2:52)

DIMENSION TWO:
WHAT DOES THE BIBLE MEAN?

As is true of the other Gospel writers, Luke wrote in Greek and clearly used the Septuagint (Greek) translation of the Old Testament (made about 250 B.C.). He was a fine Greek scholar who knew his language well. Some of Luke's poems and descriptions are unexcelled in verbal beauty. (See 1:46-55, 68-79.)

The Scripture for this first lesson is divided into six themes:
1. Preface: Writer's Purpose in Writing (1:1-4)
2. The Promise to Zechariah of the Birth of John (1:5-25)
3. The Promise to Mary of the Birth of Jesus (1:26-38)

4. The Birth of John (1:57-80)
5. The Birth of Jesus (2:1-20)
6. Jesus' Infancy and Childhood (2:21-52)

❏ *Luke 1:1-4.* The writer does not identify himself by name in either the Gospel of Luke or in the Acts of the Apostles. He refers to himself as *I* in Acts 1:1 and *me* in Luke 1:3. The early church fathers affirmed the writer as Luke, the beloved physician and companion of the apostle Paul. We accept that identification also. Greek writers usually dedicated their work to someone who had been of great significance or help to them. Theophilus seems to have been such a person for Luke. Luke wrote to this "most excellent Theophilus" in order to give him the result of his (Luke's) research into the life, teachings, and resurrection of Jesus. Some scholars suggest Luke wrote these two volumes (Luke and Acts) as legal briefs to be used by authorities (such as Theophilus?) to support Paul in his trials in Rome. Luke is cautious and sympathetic in his statements about the Roman Empire. He carefully ties Christian events to specific reigns of Roman emperors, governors, and procurators. Perhaps one of Luke's motives in writing was to make these connections. Thus his Gospel would be a strong witness to the Christian faith wherever it was read.

We are grateful that "our dear friend Luke, the doctor" (Colossians 4:14) describes his method of writing. Luke begins with certain "things that have been fulfilled among us" (concerning Jesus). He then refers to information he has from witnesses, from ministers of the word, and from the implied reading of other written documents (such as the Gospel of Mark). Then he decides to "write an orderly account" about Jesus.

Luke's description is the clearest statement by a writer in the Bible as to how he wrote his Gospel. Luke states that he primarily compiled, not composed, his book. He took his varied sources, ordered them, even corrected the grammar in some, and revised awkward sentence structures.

❏ *Luke 1:5-25.* Zechariah, a priest, was a member of the eighth of twenty-four divisions of priests. Each division was responsible for the conduct of worship in the Temple two weeks a year.

6   LUKE

King David had created these divisions (1 Chronicles 23; 24:10). In Jesus' day about seven thousand "ordinary" priests (such as Zechariah), two hundred chief priests, and one high priest were serving in the Temple. Zechariah was chosen by lot from his division to serve a week in the Temple. He was responsible for placing fresh wine and bread on a small table and also for getting incense and lighting it. The incense was a symbol that God was listening to the Jews as they prayed.

While Zechariah was performing these tasks in the holy place, God spoke to him through "an angel of the Lord." The angel said that Zechariah and his wife, Elizabeth, would be blessed by a son, whose name would be John. Because Zechariah does not believe the angel's words, he "will be silent and not able to speak" until John's birth. When John was born, Zechariah called for a tablet (since he could not speak) and wrote, "His name is John" (1:63). John would herald the Christ.

❑ *Luke 1:26-38.* In the annunciation to Mary, the angel Gabriel says, "Greetings, you who are highly favored! The Lord is with you." Gabriel's words remind me of Moses, who asked God, "How will anyone know that you are pleased with me and with your people unless you go with us? What else will distinguish me and your people from all the other people on the face of the earth?" (Exodus 33:16). Mary experiences the true Mosaic covenant anew in her life. And yet, through her, a greater covenant will come in her son. God is visiting God's people in a new way, through a young maiden whose son will be the Messiah.

"The Holy Spirit will come upon you," the angel says to Mary. "The power of the Most High will overshadow you" (Luke 1:35). Perhaps Mary thought of Genesis 1, which tells of God's hovering over the void and bringing order out of chaos. God created life where there had been none, fashioning human beings with the potential of living Godlike lives. The Holy Spirit (God's Spirit) would hover over her! A new kind of person would be brought into God's kingdom.

❑ *Luke 1:39-56.* Mary's visit to Elizabeth confirms that both women are carrying sons of great significance. Mary sings a lovely song. After Mary has been with Elizabeth for three months, the time comes for Elizabeth to be delivered of her son, John. We wonder how Mary, now six months pregnant, returned to Nazareth (over eighty miles north of Jerusalem).

❑ *Luke 1:57-80.* The statement "Her neighbors and relatives heard that the Lord had shown her great mercy" indicates the attitude of that day toward childlessness. Because of some "disgrace among the people" (1:25) Elizabeth had committed, God has refused to give her children, people assume; but now God shows mercy.

On the eighth day Zechariah and his relatives and friends participate in the ceremony of circumcision—the baby is given a physical mark of being a true son of Abraham—after which the baby is given a name. The guests want to name him after his father, Zechariah; but Elizabeth refuses: "No! He is to be called John." The guests reply that Elizabeth and Zechariah do not have a single relative named John. Zechariah, speechless since the day he questioned the angel about his and Elizabeth's having a son, motions for a tablet. On it he writes, "His name is John."

Zechariah ends his nine months of speechlessness by singing two songs, one to John (1:76-77) who would be a prophet and the other to the unborn Jesus (1:68-75, 78-79); for God has "redeemed his people" and "has raised up a horn of salvation for us / in the house of his servant David."

❑ *Luke 2:1-20.* Luke shows his love for order, specific names, dates, and places here. In these verses he gives the name of the emperor of Rome (Caesar Augustus) and of the governor of Syria (Quirinius). He also makes a statement about Caesar's order for all persons in the Empire to go to their native city to enroll in the new tax structure. Joseph and Mary go to Bethlehem. And while they are there, Mary gives birth to her first son and wraps him in cloths. She then places the newborn baby in a manger.

Soon some shepherds come to witness the good news that they have heard in the silence of their work. Perhaps these sensitive shepherds had been talking about the hoped-for coming of the Messiah. Suddenly, a great choir sang of his birth (verse 14). Mary never forgot that night.

❑ *Luke 2:21-52.* As with John three months earlier, Jesus is circumcised and given a name, *Jesus.* The rites of purification and presentation came on the fortieth day after a baby boy's birth. The presentation of the baby to God involves the father's holding the baby in his hands, arms raised to God, and dedicating him, the first-born male, to God. It is interesting to note that whereas Hannah and Elkanah presented the baby Samuel to God and left him to be trained as a helper in the house of the Lord (1 Samuel 1:22-28), Joseph and Mary redeem their son by sacrificing "a pair of doves or two young pigeons."

As a Jewish boy enters his thirteenth year, he may become a son of the covenant. The rite of his bar mitzvah shows this. At the Feast of the Passover, one of the three major festivals of Judaism, Jesus presents himself before the priests to be tested.

It is interesting to read that Joseph and Mary leave for Nazareth and are gone three days before discovering the absence of their son. Returning to the Temple, they find Jesus talking with a number of priests. When Joseph and Mary ask him where he has been and what he has been doing for the past several days, Jesus responds by saying, "Didn't you know I had to be in my Father's house?" The Greek New Testament has no noun after the word *Father's*, so the reader can add an appropriate word: my Father's house, my Father's business, purposes, concerns, or another noun.

DIMENSION THREE:
WHAT DOES THE BIBLE MEAN TO ME?

An Orderly Account

The Prologue of Luke's Gospel presents many theologically significant ideas. I find three that are compelling in my life: (1) Luke's description of how his Gospel came into being, (2) the fact of the Incarnation, and (3) the movement of the Holy Spirit in the Nativity.

First, I feel all Christians are deeply indebted to Luke for sharing with us how his Gospel came into being, especially since his two writings (the Gospel and Acts) represent one-fourth of the New Testament. Luke's emphasis on his compiling many sources together, arranging them in order, and choosing some items and excluding others for his story of the good news is exciting and helpful information.

Second, I am moved by the inevitability of the Incarnation. Luke, writing about A.D. 80 to 85, believes God became incarnate in Jesus by way of Jesus' birth. John's Gospel suggests that the Incarnation was prior to conception, by way of the eternal Logos (the Word, the ideas, the purposes of God). Mark assumes that God became incarnate in Jesus at the time of his baptism by John. Paul, writing about A.D. 50, declares that Jesus is the Messiah; since he is the "firstfruits of those who have fallen asleep" (1 Corinthians 15:20-23). Matthew agrees with Luke. What a fascinating series of answers to the question of the uniqueness of Jesus' incarnation. God entered into human history by way of a man, Jesus, for the welfare of us all.

Third, I value Luke's emphasis on the movement of the Holy Spirit throughout the Nativity. Zechariah; Elizabeth; Mary and Joseph; the aged Simeon and Anna; and, of course, the writer, Luke, all testify to the new emphasis of God's Spirit moving, as in Creation, to form a new person and a new humankind.

The Spirit of the Lord is on me, because he
has anointed me to preach good news (4:18a).

— 2 —
The Key to
Jesus' Public Ministry
Luke 3:1–4:30

DIMENSION ONE:
WHAT DOES THE BIBLE SAY?

Answer these questions by reading Luke 3

1. What two sets of dates does Luke give us for dating the ministry of John (and therefore Jesus' ministry)? (3:1-2)

2. Where is John, the son of Zechariah, when the word of God comes to him? (3:2)

3. Where does John go to preach? (3:3)

4. What does John preach? (3:3)

5. What does John say to the crowds who come to him? (3:7-9)

6. What responses does John make to three different groups that come to him? (3:10-14)

7. How does John respond to those who think he is the Messiah, the Christ? (3:15-18)

8. Why does Herod the tetrarch imprison John? (3:19-20)

9. When John baptizes Jesus, at what point (before, during, or after) does Jesus experience heaven opening before him? (3:21)

10. To whom and for whose benefit does the voice from heaven declare that Jesus is his beloved Son? (3:22)

11. How old is Jesus as he begins his ministry? (3:23)

Answer these questions by reading Luke 4:1-30

12. What leads Jesus in the desert? (4:1-2)

13. After fasting forty days, Jesus is hungry and experiences three temptations. What are these temptations? (4:3-12)

14. How does Jesus deal with these temptations? (4:4, 8, 12)

15. After the forty days in the desert, where does Jesus go? (4:14)

16. Before going to Nazareth, where does Jesus teach? (4:15)

17. Where would Jesus normally be on the sabbath? (4:16)

18. What is the scroll from which Jesus reads? (4:17)

19. To what passage of Scripture does Jesus turn? (4:18-19)

20. What does Jesus say that makes all speak well of him? (4:21)

21. What is the congregation expecting Jesus to do? (4:23)

22. How does Jesus deal with his friends' prejudices? (4:25-27)

23. What do the worshipers do to Jesus? (4:28-29)

24. How does Jesus escape? (4:30)

DIMENSION TWO:
WHAT DOES THE BIBLE MEAN?

The Scripture for this lesson is divided into four themes:

1. The Message of John the Baptist (3:1-20)
2. Jesus' Baptism and His Genealogy (3:21-38)
3. The Temptation of Jesus (4:1-13)
4. Jesus' Declaration of His Messiahship (4:14-30)

❑ *Luke 3:1-20.* Luke gives us data from two sets of dates for determining the year both John and Jesus began their ministries. The year is A.D. 28–29. The first set of dates comes from the secular world: Tiberius Caesar is emperor of the Roman Empire. Tiberius was elected to that position by the Roman Senate in August, A.D. 14. His first year was August, A.D. 14 to August, A.D. 15. Adding Luke's fifteenth year to fourteen gives us the period of time A.D. 28–29.

Besides the above date, Luke says Pontius Pilate was governor of Judea during this time. He held office from A.D. 26 to 36. Three tetrarchs, half-brothers from the house of Herod, were ruling in various places in Palestine and Lebanon during the time of Jesus and John.

The religious dates Luke gives refer to the house of Annas, who was a powerful and rich high priest who purchased his priesthood from Rome and dominated priestly activities and politics. Annas saw to it that his son-in-law Caiaphas was high priest from A.D. 16 to 36.

The crowds in verse 10 probably include religious teachers—the rabbis and priests who were responsible for religious teaching in the law. John scorns them because they assume their lineage in Abraham will save them. John declares (in our language), Not roots, but fruits!

The tax collectors (verse 12) are those who greedily purchase the financial privilege of sitting at various customs centers to collect revenue from caravans and persons transporting goods from one province to another. Matthew represents such a tax collector. The soldiers (verse 14) are non-Jewish men in the Roman army of occupation. Rome excused Jews from military service.

John tells these groups to share what they have with those who have not, to use their powers of authority with justice and kindness, and not to extort or take what is not theirs by violence.

John's message is founded on the apocalyptic idea of the coming kingdom; that is, humankind is so evil and pagan that believers can do nothing to change the world. Only God can and will do so, by sending the long-awaited Messiah who will bring the judgment of God. The metaphors John uses in verse 17 are those of the autumnal harvest festival—scenes of the separation of grain and chaff, of good and no-good (evil), of burning the chaff. Jesus considers John less than the "least in the kingdom of God" (7:26-28), for John does not preach the good news that changed lives will help bring the rule of God on earth. John calls for repentance so people can be saved from the fires of judgment. Jesus calls people to learn of the loving God who wants human beings to seek the fullness of life through living lives of justice, kindness, mercy, unselfishness, and good will. The two views (apocalypse and prophecy) both use the term *kingdom of God*; but the intention, purpose, and means of ushering in the Kingdom in each view are "miles apart."

❑ *Luke 3:21-28.* Jesus left Nazareth and was baptized by John. Jesus was baptized, ancient traditions claim, not because he had sinned, but because he wanted to be an acknowledged participant in the kingdom of God. After Jesus is baptized and *while he is praying*, the Holy Spirit comes upon Jesus and he hears God speaking to him: "You are my son, whom I love; with you I am well pleased." This is Jesus' personal experience of being called to messiahship. Matthew's account assumes the voice is making a public announcement; Luke makes it personal.

❑ *Luke 4:1-13.* Luke states that Jesus was led by the Spirit for forty days in the desert and was tempted by the devil. After nearly six weeks of mental and spiritual stress and strain as he sought the meaning of what God wanted him to be as the Messiah, Jesus then realized how hungry he was and what hunger means to countless thousands. Then it was that Jesus' messianic consciousness was interpreted in terms of human needs. He was tempted to turn stones to bread (for himself and for others), to experience the accolade of the crowds in recognition of uniqueness and greatness, and to use his personal powers and authority to gain righteousness throughout the world.

None of the temptations was based on gross evil. Jesus was not tempted to steal; kill; lie; commit adultery; or sell his soul for greed, hate, jealousy, selfishness. His temptations were on a high moral level. For example, he would not choose the better if the best were known: Jesus would refuse to fulfill the Pharisees' messianic hope of legalistic obedience to the oral traditions of the law (such as never helping a sick person receive healing on the sabbath); Jesus would refuse to fulfill the Zealots' messianic hopes of creating a great army and leading them in destroying the Roman forces in order to gain a new Jerusalem; Jesus would refuse to submit to the priests' (Sadducees) belief that complete obedience to all priestly rituals, festivals, functions, and Torah would make persons just, kind, unselfish, loving; Jesus could not join in the Herodian concept that the nation can produce peace by simply giving in to whatever those in power want you to do.

Jesus was a revolutionary in his ministry. His mission would require disagreement with John the Baptist's emphasis on an apocalyptic Messiah—a heavenly Messiah coming to earth on a great white military horse, leading a vast corps of militant angels who were descending to earth to save the believers and to destroy those who were evil. This hope of a prophet-priest-king Messiah could not be incorporated into Jesus' experiences.

❑ *Luke 4:14-30.* This passage emphasizes the importance of the Holy Spirit in the life of Jesus. Jesus' mother (Mary), Elizabeth, and Joseph had experienced the Holy Spirit in their lives. Jesus experiences the Holy Spirit coming upon him at baptism; leading him to the wilderness; and now after six weeks in the wilderness, leading him into Galilee.

Jesus preached his first sermon in Nazareth at his home synagogue. At first he was well received. Then he began to "meddle" with the prayer life of the adult males. He knew every male had prayed at home the usual morning prayers, which thanked God he was not a Gentile, a woman, or a slave (or, as some have suggested, a leper). Jesus used his Bible (the writings of the Former Prophets) to show that God holds no prejudice against women, Gentiles, or slaves (or lepers). Jesus refers to Elijah being sent by God during a long famine, not to Israelite women, but to a Gentile woman whom he fed (1 Kings 17:8-16). Jesus refers to how Elisha through God had saved Naaman, a commanding officer of the hated Syrian army—a Gentile who had leprosy, as was true of many Jews in Israel at that time (2 Kings 5:1-14). The Scripture shows that God loves Gentiles, even Gentile women and a leprous Gentile military officer. No one in the synagogue could dispute this truth.

Jesus read from Isaiah 61:1-2, which states the "program" or goals of the prophet on whom the Holy Spirit would come. Each is a challenge to gain a new religious perspective and high ethical concern for all God's children, regardless of their status in life—poor, outcast, imprisoned (physically, mentally, psychologically, and spiritually), oppressed, blind. God cares about all people, regardless of sex, race, or status.

DIMENSION THREE:
WHAT DOES THE BIBLE MEAN TO ME?

Luke 4:18-21—New Understanding of the Kingdom

This passage of Scripture is one of the most important in the New Testament. The key to Jesus' public and personal ministry is found here. The keys to our own understanding as followers of the Christ, as disciples of Christ, are here as well.

First, we see Jesus being reaffirmed as the Son of God by the Holy Spirit at the baptism of John. Judaism was waiting for this great event. Jesus' forty days in the wilderness firmly fixed in Jesus' mind the kind of Messiah God wanted him to be—and what he was not to be! Even the genealogy speaks volumes: Jesus is the son of David, but he is also a descendant (or brother) of Adam (that is, of humankind). Jesus is related to people of all races.

Jesus resolved the meaning of messiahship, declaring what he could not identify with (as with the Pharisees and scribes, Herodians, Zealots, Essenes, Sadducees). He would so live that persons who saw him would know that the Spirit of God was within him, kindling his moral sensitivities, mental comprehension of truth, and his love for all people. In short, his message was revolutionary in theology; in psychology; and in social attitudes related to racism, feminism, and religious pride in the prayer life of a typical male Jew.

Where John wanted the Messiah to baptize with the Holy Spirit and with fire (of judgment), Jesus baptized with the Holy Spirit of love and with the burning fire within the heart. Jesus brought a new understanding of the kingdom of God.

I have not come to call the righteous, but sinners to repentance (5:32).

—— 3 ——

Jesus' Galilean Ministry

Luke 4:31–6:49

DIMENSION ONE:
WHAT DOES THE BIBLE SAY?

Answer these questions by reading Luke 4:31-44

1. Where does Jesus go after he leaves Nazareth? (4:31)

2. While in the synagogue, a man verbally accosts Jesus. What is the man's problem? (4:33-34)

3. What does Jesus say to the demon? (4:35)

4. Whose mother-in-law does Jesus cure, and what does she do after Jesus cures her? (4:38-39)

5. Whom does Jesus heal? (4:40-41)

6. Where does Jesus go the next morning, and what does he say he must do? (4:42-43)

7. In what country is Jesus preaching? (4:44)

Answer these questions by reading Luke 5:1-11

8. How many boats does Jesus see by the shore, and to whom do they belong? (5:2-3)

9. From whose boat does Jesus speak? (5:3)

10. After teaching the people, what does Jesus tell Simon to do? (5:4)

11. Why does Simon signal to his partners to bring their boat, and what are the results? (5:6-7)

12. What does Simon Peter do? (5:8)

13. Who are Jesus' first disciples? (5:10-11)

Answer these questions by reading Luke 5:12–6:11

14. What does a person suffering from leprosy beg Jesus to do? (5:12)

15. How does Jesus respond to the plea of the person suffering from leprosy? (5:13)

16. What three things happen next? (5:13-14)

17. Why does Jesus forgive the sins of the paralyzed man? (5:19-20)

18. Why do the teachers of the law and the Pharisees question Jesus' words? (5:21)

19. Who becomes the next disciple, and what does he do to honor Jesus? (5:27-29)

20. What is Jesus' reply to the Pharisees and teachers of the law as to why he and his disciples do not fast? (5:33-34)

21. After a night in prayer, Jesus called his disciples and "chose twelve of them, whom he also designated apostles." Who are the Twelve? (6:12-16)

22. What are Luke's four Beatitudes? (6:20-22)

23. What does Jesus say about behavior toward enemies? (6:27-28)

24. What is the reward for this behavior? (6:35)

25. What is Jesus' test of goodness? (6:43-45)

26. Everyone who hears and does Jesus' words is like a man who builds his house in a certain way. How does he build it? (6:48)

DIMENSION TWO:
WHAT DOES THE BIBLE MEAN?

The Scripture for this lesson, describing the Galilean ministry, is divided into four themes:

1. Healings in Capernaum, Time of Reflection (4:31-44)
2. Jesus Makes His First Disciples (5:1-11)

3. Healings and Confrontations (5:12–6:11)
4. The Great Sermon (6:12-49)

❑ *Luke 4:31-44.* Luke, who was writing for non-Jewish persons unacquainted with the topography of Palestine, correctly states that Jesus "went down" to Capernaum. From Nazareth to Capernaum is a drop of approximately 2,600 feet. Capernaum, well below sea level, is usually a hot place during the daytime but has wonderful breezes from the Sea of Galilee during the night.

Jesus teaches in the synagogue in Capernaum. What Jesus says was not new in terms of content or rhetorical form but in terms of the authority with which he spoke. Luke 5:31-32 and 6:43-44 reveal Jesus' healing power and authority of preaching. Members of the synagogue are "amazed" at his teaching and preaching; for Jesus speaks with personal authority, not depending on the interpretations of learned rabbis through the centuries.

A man "possessed by a demon, an evil spirit," cries out at Jesus. He assumes that Jesus ("the Holy One of God") will destroy his way of life. Jesus rebukes the evil within him.

Though Simon is not yet a disciple, he must have valued Jesus' presence greatly; for he offers his home to Jesus as the center for his ministry in Galilee. Luke says "they" asked Jesus to heal her. Who makes up the "they"? "They" is probably Simon, his wife, and Andrew (see Mark 1:29). Jesus stands at the head of the bed ("over her") and rebukes the fever. "And it left her."

❑ *Luke 5:1-11.* We mentioned above that Jesus knows Simon, whose brother is Andrew; and Jesus would also know their fishing partners, James and John. As Jesus stands by the Lake of Gennesaret (that is, by the Sea of Galilee), he is aware of the pressing crowds who want to hear him. Seeing the two fishing boats, Jesus goes to Simon's boat and climbs aboard. Jesus is now free from the press of the crowd, and he begins to teach. Notice that Jesus, as when he preached in Nazareth, sits down (see Luke 4:20).

When Jesus finishes, knowing that his good friends Simon and Andrew have fished fruitlessly all night, he tells Simon to "put out into deep water, and let down the nets for a catch." Then comes the astonishing catch of a shoal of fish—so great that "they" (Simon and Andrew) signal to their partners, James and John, to help. Both boats fill with fish. Simon's reaction is astonishment (5:9) and at least a hint of an understanding of Jesus as the Messiah.

Luke's account records the early church's memory of the call of the first and most important disciple, Simon Peter. From an ordinary fisherman will come an extraordinary fisher of persons.

❑ *Luke 5:12-16.* The story of Jesus touching a person suffering from leprosy is first told in the Gospel of Mark (1:40-45), which is the basic account used by both Matthew (8:1-4) and Luke (5:12-16). Both Matthew and Mark state that the person suffering from leprosy came and knelt before Jesus; Luke says that the person suffering from leprosy "fell with his face to the ground," meaning he worshiped him. The person suffering from leprosy begs Jesus to heal him: "If you are willing, you can make me clean."

This incident occurs at the beginning of Jesus' ministry. To touch a disfigured and sin-scarred person suffering from leprosy would make him unclean in the eyes of the Pharisees, Sadducees, and teachers of the law! Jesus lays his mission on the line when he lovingly, though perhaps with considerable emotional tension, reaches out and touches the man covered with leprosy. Love wins out. The person suffering from leprosy is cleansed, and Jesus' messianic mission is defined.

No wonder Jesus withdraws to lonely places and prays. For one thing, he wants that sense of at-one-ment with the Father. He wants assurance that he has chosen, not just the *good*, but the *best*—with concern for persons always being the highest priority.

❑ *Luke 5:17-26.* The story of the paralyzed man falls in the category of a healing miracle. Jesus simply says, "Your sins are forgiven. . . . Get up, take your mat and go home." And the man does. Jesus angers some religious leaders because he offers forgiveness of sins. Only God can forgive sins, they argue. The scribes and the Pharisees put theological doctrine

24   LUKE

above loving action for those in need. Jesus demonstrates God's love for sinners.

❏ *Luke 5:33-39.* The "new" is the message of Jesus. It is natural for people to stick with old ways of life rather than to be open to the new call of Jesus.

❏ *Luke 6:1-5.* Another source of contention between Jesus and some of the Pharisees is the question of obedience to the laws of the sabbath. The Pharisees do not feel that Jesus is obeying those laws. Yet the great King David had showed more concern for feeding his hungry men than for obeying ritualistic regulations.

❏ *Luke 6:12-49.* The opening word of the Beatitudes in Matthew, Mark, and Luke is *blessed.* It has been translated a number of different ways, such as happy, fortunate, lucky. I suggest the root meaning refers to a person who has had the privilege of kneeling in the presence of his king (David or Solomon) or the King of kings (God or Jesus Christ). I know of no other word that catches up the nuances of the psychological and spiritual status of such a person. Persons who have been in the presence of true greatness, that is, those who have been "blessed" of God, may be among the economically poor of their day. They are rich in the jewels of the spirit but poor in material things. The character of their lives is not determined by how many things they possess. They are rich toward God. The Beatitudes are not merely a promise but an invitation to the kingdom of God.

DIMENSION THREE:
WHAT DOES THE BIBLE MEAN TO ME?

Luke 6:20-26—Blessings and Woes

Let us look more closely at the word *blessed.* It carries a wealth of beautiful meaning for us. Have you ever heard a person say, "I really got my dander up and blessed him out good and proper"? What did the person mean by "blessed him out"?

The meaning has an interesting Hebrew origin. Do you recall the biblical story of Balaam (Numbers 22–24)? King

Balak of Moab employs the pagan Gentile Balaam to go southward until he faces the intruding Israelites, who are on their way from Egypt to the Promised Land. Balak wants Balaam to curse the invaders (Israel). The story tells how Balaam, a soothsayer and occultist, is ready to curse Israel. But his curse turns into blessing. This change is easily done in Hebrew; for the same word (as is the case in English) may mean curse or blessing, depending on one's tone of voice. Instead of "blessing them out," Balaam chooses to "bless" them.

Three consonants form the Hebrew word we translate as *blessed*: BRK. As a noun, it means knee; as a verb, it means kneel down (as camels do or as subjects do before their king). One who has experienced kneeling before the Supreme Being is a "blessed" person. So how ought we to think of the phrase, "Blessed are you who are poor"? Reread the four Beatitudes in Luke and the nine in Matthew for a challenging experience of faith and love. Are the Beatitudes themselves a general guarantee of eternal bliss? Can you think of experiences in your life that encourage you to believe in blessings or woes?

The blind receive sight, the lame walk,
those who have leprosy are cured, the deaf hear,
the dead are raised, and the good news
is preached to the poor (7:22).

—— 4 ——
Jesus: Messianic Teacher and Healer
Luke 7–8

DIMENSION ONE:
WHAT DOES THE BIBLE SAY?

Answer these questions by reading Luke 7

1. Who owns a servant who is at the point of death? (7:2)

2. What does the centurion do to save the servant? (7:3)

3. Why do the elders help the centurion? (7:4-5)

4. Why does the centurion send another delegation to Jesus, suggesting that he not come? (7:6)

5. What does the centurion suggest instead? (7:7)

6. What happens? (7:10)

7. As Jesus and a large crowd approach the city gates of Nain, what event is taking place? (7:11-12)

8. How does Jesus respond? (Luke 7:13-14)

9. What does the crowd do and say after the man revives? (7:16)

10. What question does John the Baptist have two of his disciples ask Jesus? (7:19)

11. What happens "at that very time" that is a nonverbal answer to John's question? (7:21)

12. What is Jesus' verbal response to John? (7:22)

13. What is Jesus' conviction about the importance of John the Baptist? (7:28)

14. What kind of woman comes to Jesus while he dines as the guest of a Pharisee? (7:37)

15. What does she do that upsets the host? (7:38-39)

16. What does Jesus say in response to the woman's actions? (7:47)

Answer these questions by reading Luke 8

17. What part do certain women play in the daily life of Jesus and his disciples? (8:1-3)

18. In the parable of the sower, a sower sows his seed on four kinds of soil. What are these four kinds? (8:5-8)

19. Why does Jesus teach using parables? (8:9-10)

20. What is the purpose of good soil? (8:15)

21. What is the purpose of a lighted lamp? (8:16)

22. Who does Jesus say are his real relatives? (8:19-21)

23. When Jesus rebukes his disciples during a great storm on the Lake of Gennesaret (Sea of Galilee), what does he say? (8:25)

24. After Jesus cures the uncontrollable demon-possessed man, what do the townspeople find the healed man doing? (8:35b)

25. What happens to Jairus's daughter? (8:40-42, 49-56)

DIMENSION TWO: WHAT DOES THE BIBLE MEAN?

The Scripture for this lesson is divided into four themes:

1. Jesus Gives Life to Two Persons (7:1-17)
2. Jesus and John the Baptist (7:18-35)
3. Jesus and a Penitent Sinner (7:36-50)
4. Jesus as Teacher and Miracle Worker (8:1-56)

❑ *Luke 7:1-17.* After teaching "all this," Jesus returns to Capernaum. A centurion (a title given to a commanding officer of one hundred soldiers) who has a servant who is dying sends a group of Jewish elders to Jesus to ask him to come to his house and heal his servant. The elders highly recommend the centurion to Jesus and point out how much the officer "loves our nation" by saying he had financed the building of their synagogue. Jesus goes with the elders. On the way, they meet some of the centurion's friends who report that the centurion feels unworthy to have Jesus come to his house. Instead of coming, he asks Jesus only to "say the word."

The faith of the officer moves Jesus. The centurion's faith cures his servant. Luke wants us to notice that Jesus does not need to be present to perform this healing. In fact, Jesus does not even say a word!

Another healing miracle (7:11-17) takes place at the gate of the city of Nain. Jesus sees a funeral procession. The young man who died is an only son, and his mother is a widow. Jesus stops the crowd of mourners by touching the coffin. He says, "Young man, I say to you, get up!" The young man sits up, begins to speak, and Jesus gives him to his mother.

No one in the crowd says, "The Messiah has come!" Rather, they say, "A great prophet has appeared among us." Jesus would be pleased, since he does not want to be known as the Messiah who functions as a miracle worker.

❑ *Luke 7:18-35.* Meanwhile, John is still in prison. Two of John's disciples had followed Jesus after hearing John refer to him as "the Lamb of God" (John 1:36-37). Now John wonders whether Jesus is the Messiah. Jesus has not functioned as John expected him to, so John sends two of his disciples to ask Jesus, "Are you the one who was to come?"

Jesus does not answer yes or no. "At that very time" Jesus demonstrates that he is the Messiah, the *prophetic* Messiah. Jesus illustrates how the prophetic roles of Isaiah 29:18-19; 35:5-6; 61:1 are being fulfilled through him (Luke 7:18-22). Jesus even expresses his hope that John will not be offended by him.

After John's disciples leave, Jesus gives strong support to the words of John the Baptist. John is no slender reed, subject to every wind that blows; nor does he seek to clothe himself in fine courtly raiment. John is a prophet, and his prophetic mantle symbolizes that fact.

Jesus notes the two basic groups in his audience: the common people (who have been baptized by John) and the Pharisees and scribes (who denied John's ministry and now that of Jesus). John preached the judgment of God: Evildoers will suffer and be destroyed. Jesus preaches the love, kindness, and justice that God offers to save evildoers.

The two groups are like children playing. One group wants to "play wedding" and have a good time; the other group wants to play "funeral," sing dirges, and talk of fasting. The two groups cannot get together. Jesus hopes the disciples of John, the Pharisees, and the teachers of the law will join him in rejoicing, dining, drinking, and enjoying an abundant life. The invitation was and is open to all.

❑ *Luke 7:36-50.* The story of the Pharisee and the woman "who had lived a sinful life" (probably a prostitute) is a study in contrasts. The Pharisee is proud of his loyalty to religious ideals, yet he is a discourteous and thoughtless host. The woman is humble and seeks only to express her appreciation for what Jesus has meant to her.

The host, probably with sarcasm, makes a remark about the woman "who had lived a sinful life in that town" (7:37). "If this man were a prophet, he would know who is touching him and what kind of woman she is" (7:39). We might question the Pharisee's understanding of what a prophet is. Jesus is not a palm reader, a soothsayer, or a warlock. *Prophet* means "one who announces."

Jesus tells Simon (the Pharisee) a parable about a creditor who has two debtors. One is deeply in debt; the other owes but little. When the date comes to pay their debts in full, neither can do so. The creditor is a great man and forgives both men their debts. The question is, Which of the debtors will love the creditor more? The Pharisee answers (with a begrudging tone?), "I suppose the one who had the bigger debt canceled." Right. "Do you see this woman?" What a question! The Pharisee sees only a prostitute. It never occurs to him to ask, Why is she weeping? Why is she using her hair to wipe his feet? Why pour expensive oil on his feet? Jesus asks in effect, Do you really *see* this woman? If so, you see her emotions of gratitude, joy, exultation. You see her giving something to express her deep feelings about a transforming experience in her life. Sir, she has been a sinner; and I tell you that her sins, which are many, are forgiven.

How the woman must have yearned to embrace this man who had read her thoughts and expressed them so well. Under his benediction, she goes in peace and wholeness that night.

❑ *Luke 8:1-21.* Some of the women minister to Jesus and the disciples "out of their own means" (8:3). Without their support, Jesus' ministry would have been severely curtailed.

The parable of the sower is really a parable of four kinds of soil and (by metaphor) four kinds of minds:

1. Some seed falls on hard-trodden paths, so birds come and pick it up—hearers do not receive the word.

2. Some seed falls on a shallow covering of soil over solid rock, so no nourishing moisture or roots support growth—hearers lack depth.

3. Some seed falls on cultivated soil but grows up with thorns and weeds that choke its growth, so no fruit matures—hearers respond, but other interests absorb their thought life; new ideals and obligations are choked or checked, and nothing results.

4. Some seed falls on good, cultivated soil—hearers let the word grow in their ethical, moral, and spiritual systems. Their minds are open to receive new teaching, to test and try it, to live by it, and to reproduce it.

❑ *Luke 8:22-56.* Another miracle story Luke tells is that of Jesus' stilling the storm and stilling the fears of the disciples (8:22-25). Equally important, if not more so, is the next story, the story of the healing of a wild, uncontrollable, frightening, and frightened man (8:26-33). Perhaps this disturbed man had learned of the quieting of the winds in the storm and its effect on the men in the boat. Maybe he ran from the top of the high hill (where he lived among tombs) to meet Jesus, who had quieted the storm and the men. Perhaps Jesus could quiet his mind, too.

The man tells Jesus that his name is *Legion* (a term for a division of six thousand soldiers), for he felt his mind was all too often like a huge mob. He does not know which values should be primary in his life. Soon, Legion is "sitting at Jesus' feet, dressed [for he had been naked] and in his right mind" (8:35). The man finds a new and more suitable life through the life of Jesus.

Luke tells of two healing miracles in 8:40-56—one about a young girl of twelve and the other about a woman who has suffered for twelve years. In desperation, the woman dares to touch Jesus' outer garment. Jesus, even though in the midst of a crowd, feels the touch and says, "Someone touched me; I know that power has gone out from me." And she is healed immediately by her touch of faith.

The daughter of one of the rulers of the synagogue has a similar miracle experience when Jesus takes her by her hand, saying, "My child, get up!" and she gets up.

Even today a power is channeled from God through Jesus Christ to those receiving it. I bear witness to such power being conveyed to my year-old granddaughter. She was clinically dead (no heartbeat or breathing for twenty minutes). She was revived and is fully alive today because of the miracle of the flow of healing power from the Master.

DIMENSION THREE:
WHAT DOES THE BIBLE MEAN TO ME?

Luke 8:9-10—Insiders

One of the most thought-provoking passages in this lesson is drawn from Luke 8:9-10. We do not know the context in which Jesus made the enigmatic statements. Perhaps it was a time when Jesus felt that the average person misses so much that God has to offer. Persons see, but they do not see; they hear, but they do not hear; they feel, but they do not feel. Some certainly hear, and their hearts sing with hallelujahs. Some see with stereoscopic vision—they see the obvious and more. What they see includes the omniscient and loving God. Faith helps us see more than the obvious.

The psalmist sang, "The heavens declare the glory of God; / the skies proclaim the work of his hands" (Psalm 19:1). Today astronomers have more ways of seeing the starry heavens and more reasons for exultation as they observe our galaxy and millions of other galaxies. Through their radio telescopes they have seen (a billion light years out in space) evidence of the same basic elements for producing life as on earth: oxygen, hydrogen, potassium, amino acids, protein, sugar. But some persons fail to see more than matter. They fail to see God. They rejoice only in what nature has produced. They see but fail to see.

*"Who do you say I am?" Peter answered,
"The Christ of God" (9:20).*

— 5 —

The Disciples Accept Jesus as Messiah

Luke 9:1-50

DIMENSION ONE:
WHAT DOES THE BIBLE SAY?

Answer these questions by reading Luke 9:1-17

1. Before Jesus sends "the Twelve" on their first mission, what does he give them? (9:1)

2. What does Jesus send them out to do? (9:2)

3. What rules does Jesus give for their journey? (9:3-5)

4. What does Herod hear and think about these missions? (9:7)

5. What political leader "tried to see" Jesus? (9:9)

6. After the disciples report to Jesus on their mission, where does Jesus take them? (9:10)

7. When the crowds search for and find Jesus at Bethsaida, where he and his disciples have withdrawn for a spiritual retreat, what does Jesus do? (9:11)

8. Late in the afternoon, what do the disciples ask Jesus to do? (9:12)

9. What does Jesus say to the Twelve? (9:13)

10. After the disciples tell Jesus they have only five loaves and two fish, what does Jesus do? (9:14b-16)

11. How many persons partake of this meal, and how much food is left over? (9:14a-17)

Answer these questions by reading Luke 9:18-27

12. What responses does Jesus receive when he asks who people say he is? (9:18-19)

13. What response does Jesus receive when he asks, "Who do you say I am?" (9:20)

14. What command does Jesus then give the disciples? (9:21-22)

15. What must a person do to be Jesus' disciple? (9:23)

Answer these questions by reading Luke 9:28-43a

16. Eight days later, what happens to Jesus on the mountain, where he goes to pray? (9:28-30)

17. Who does Jesus take to the mountain with him? (9:28)

18. What proposal does Peter make to Jesus? (9:33)

19. What is the significance of the cloud? (9:34-35)

20. When the voice (of God) finishes speaking, who is left on the mountain? (9:36)

21. When Jesus, Peter, James, and John come down the mountain to the valley, who meets them? (9:37-39)

22. Who has tried to heal the boy suffering from convulsions? (9:40)

23. What does Jesus do? (9:42b)

Answer these questions by reading Luke 9:43b-50

24. While everyone is "marveling at all that Jesus did," what prediction does Jesus make of his Passion? (9:44)

25. While Jesus tries to inform his disciples about his interpretation of the messianic hope, in what argument do the disciples engage? (9:46)

DIMENSION TWO:
WHAT DOES THE BIBLE MEAN?

The Scripture for this lesson, describing when, where, and how the twelve disciples finally accepted Jesus as the Messiah (Christ), is divided into five themes:

1. Jesus Directs His Disciples in Mission (9:1-11)
2. The Feeding of the Five Thousand (9:12-17)
3. Peter's Confession and the First Prediction of Jesus' Passion (9:18-27)

4. The Transfiguration and Curing a Boy With Epilepsy (9:28-43a)
5. The Second Prediction of Jesus' Passion and a Pagan Exorcist (9:43b-50)

❑ *Luke 9:1-11.* When Jesus called the twelve disciples, he wanted men who were willing to give time and effort to being trained in his mission. Jesus chose the Twelve from hundreds of possibilities. The Twelve would go into various parts of the world to represent him. They would speak with his passion, conviction, insights, parables. Having listened to his teachings, they would "be sent" (which is the meaning of the word *apostle*) in place of Jesus. They undoubtedly repeated scores of his most "successful" stories (parables). Later, many of these would be recorded (as was done by the compilers of the Gospels of Matthew, Mark, and Luke).

It would be fascinating to know how each of the Twelve responded when they realized they were to teach and preach in the place of Jesus. Their status as disciples ("learners who sit at the feet of a teacher") changed considerably when Jesus told them they would go as disciples to do what he had been doing, namely, exorcise unclean spirits, heal the diseased, and preach his word of the kingdom of God. They are no longer just listeners, they are participants. This is true in our day too; all Christians are in the ministry of Jesus Christ. We are given the "power and authority" to act in his name.

Jesus set up some "rules for the journey," which are listed in 9:4-5. The next unit of Scripture, dealing with Herod Antipas (9:7-9), sets the tone for this chapter. The basic question Herod raises is, "Who, then, is this I hear such things about?" The "such things" would have included what the six teams (as Mark 6:7 states about the Twelve) achieved on their first mission. They reported to Jesus about their experiences—some of which Herod "needed" to know about, since they have invaded a number of villages and cities in his tetrarchy (Galilee). In fact, Herod "tried to see him [Jesus]."

Recall that Herod had ordered the beheading of John the Baptist (at the request of Salome, daughter of Herodias by an earlier husband, Philip). Luke does not press this fact, for Luke considers the important thing about Herod to be his desire to hear and see Jesus.

But we should note that Herod Antipas's father (Herod the Great) is said to have killed male babies in Bethlehem, thinking a baby of the tribe of David living in Bethlehem might well be a political challenge to his power.

So, Luke is interested, not in what Herod Antipas thinks about John or even what he thinks about Elijah, but what he thinks about this man who "gives power and authority" to others in his name. Herod Antipas has the power, doesn't he? What of this man who is granting power to others?

Someone has said, "Bad people have no more trouble in believing the creeds than good people." Herod Antipas was like that. The Herod family had been forcibly converted over a century before; they heard and (verbally) accepted the Jewish creeds but never acted out their faith.

❏ *Luke 9:12-17.* Jesus and his twelve disciples are in Bethsaida ("house of fishers") for what we would call a "spiritual retreat." While they are sharing their experiences (with occasional suggestions or probings from Jesus?), a large crowd finds them. The village of Bethsaida had been rebuilt by the tetrarch Philip to become his capital. Jesus considered it a pagan city and condemned it (10:13). So the crowd leaves the boundaries of Galilee and crosses eastward to the territory of Philip.

At day's end the disciples suggest to Jesus that he send them in search of housing and food. Jesus looks at them and suggests, "You give them something to eat." To feed five thousand men (plus their families?)—what a miracle that would be! The disciples count up their store of food: five loaves and two fish. After the disciples divide the five thousand into groups of about fifty each, Jesus takes the bread, looks toward heaven (as all Jewish fathers did at mealtime), and thanks God for the food. He then "gave them to the disciples to set before the people." If you take "set before the people" literally, the twelve "ushers" took the meal of five loaves and two fish throughout the area. None of the Synoptic Gospels suggests that Jesus multiplied the elements (fish and bread). What did happen? We do not know. But we are told by all the Gospels that everyone had plenty for dinner that evening, and there were twelve baskets of food left. A miracle had happened!

❑ *Luke 9:18-27.* Not only Herod Antipas wants to know who "this" (Jesus) is, Jesus wants to know if his disciples know who he is! Jesus takes his disciples with him to pray. After prayer he asks them who people say he is. Some say John the Baptist (revived); others say Elijah; still others say that "one of the prophets of long ago has come back to life." "But who do you say that I am?" Peter answers, "The Christ of God." Luke uses the Greek word for Messiah: Christ. Jesus, with implicit agreement, commands that they tell no one! Then he says that he "must suffer many things and be rejected by the elders, chief priests and teachers of the law, and he must be killed and on the third day be raised to life" (9:22). From this point on Jesus reinterprets the messianic hope (which he spearheads) in terms of service, suffering, and sacrifice. His model is the suffering servant.

❑ *Luke 9:28-43a.* About eight days later, Jesus and his three closest (perhaps most spiritually akin) disciples go up a high mountain (probably Mount Tabor, south of Nazareth) to pray. As Jesus prays, he experiences the presence of Israel's lawgiver, Moses, and one of Israel's early prophetic leaders, Elijah.

The lawgiver and charismatic prophet appear here with Jesus, perhaps in a kind of consultative capacity to him. Jesus already knows who he is (the Messiah). But the three disciples acknowledged this claim only recently. Now, through the transfiguration of Jesus, they have even greater support. They too experience the presence of Moses and Elijah and what they symbolize in Judaism. The presence of the living spirits of Moses and Elijah, with the obvious support they were giving Jesus, must have transformed the minds and spirits of the three disciples as much as it transfigured the body of Jesus.

When Jesus and the three disciples come down from the mountain, Jesus expresses God's love by healing a boy suffering from epilepsy.

❑ *Luke 9:43b-50.* While there is no problem with what Jesus does, there is a problem of understanding what he says. Neither his chosen Twelve (the apostles) nor his many followers understood his interpretations of messiahship. Hence, he says,

THE DISCIPLES ACCEPT JESUS AS MESSIAH

You must "listen carefully to what I am about to tell you: The Son of Man [Jesus] is going to be betrayed into the hands of men." Jesus seeks to let them know he will suffer and will be rebuffed by the religious leaders of Jerusalem.

John raises a question when he sees a "non-Christian" exorcist "driving out" demons (unclean spirits) from persons. John has trouble with this good deed because the man does not belong to the company Jesus leads. So John forbids the man to heal, especially since he does so in the name of Jesus. Jesus responds by saying, "Whoever is not against you is for you."

DIMENSION THREE:
WHAT DOES THE BIBLE MEAN TO ME?

Seeing God Through Jesus

One of the most transforming revelations is to imagine the transfigured Jesus leaving the mountain peak to go to the valley as the compassionate healer of a boy. Empathize with this unique and superior human being, bending down to hear the human cry of a father whose only child, a son, has epilepsy. Does God (and his Messiah) care about such a boy?

The question is ridiculous to a convert. But it is unbelievable to many. Jesus had taken three disciples with him to Mount Tabor. The other nine stayed in the valley, preaching and healing. When the man with an epileptic son sought help, they tried to minister in Jesus' name; but they could not do so successfully in this case. Jesus, returning from a major divine revelation of his identity (as the Messiah), cures the boy. "And they were all amazed at the greatness of God." This phrase is a beautiful expression of the fact that persons may see God through Jesus Christ.

Think of the many ways you are astonished at the majesty of God through Jesus. Begin with the expectations of the Jews for a Messiah. Add announcement and birth stories and the story of a youth of twelve asking questions of the religious leaders at the Temple. Next, list John the Baptist preaching a baptism of repentance for the forgiveness of sins in the wilderness. Other ways include: the innumerable parables that describe God in nontheological vocabulary, the magnificent lifestyle that won converts who have responded so favorably to the majesty of God, and Jesus' amazing ability to receive the painful venom of those who hate him and turn a loving countenance toward them and forgive them. They did not know who he was or what he offered.

Another challenge (from 9:45) is our need continually to pray for understanding of Jesus' reinterpretation of the kingdom of God. We should never cease learning. It has been said that the "absence of comprehension can sometimes have consequences as disastrous as the actual presence of evil purpose" (*The Interpreter's Bible*, Vol. 8; Abingdon Press, 1952; page 178).

I am convinced that the false prophets (of both Old Testament times and our own) are not those who are insincere, not those who are unconcerned. They are false prophets because they are not informed; they lack the necessary knowledge. As Hosea put it, "My people are destroyed from lack of knowledge" (Hosea 4:6).

Follow me (9:59a).

—— 6 ——

Jesus Sets His Face Toward Jerusalem

Luke 9:51–11:36

DIMENSION ONE:
WHAT DOES THE BIBLE SAY?

Answer these questions by reading Luke 9:51-62

1. To what city does Jesus "resolutely set out"? (9:51)

2. Before going to a Samaritan village, what does Jesus do? (9:52)

3. How does Jesus respond to James and John, who want to destroy the Samaritans who refuse to receive him? (9:55-56)

4. When a man says, "I will follow you wherever you go" (9:57), what is Jesus' response? (9:58)

5. Another man says, "Lord, first let me go and bury my father" (9:59). What is Jesus' response? (9:60)

6. A third man says, "First let me go back and say good-by to my family" (9:61). What is Jesus' response? (9:62)

Answer these questions by reading Luke 10

7. How many followers does Jesus appoint to send into every town and place? (10:1)

8. If a town does not receive them, what are they to say? (10:11)

9. What reports do the seventy-two make to Jesus? (10:17)

10. What is Jesus' response to their joyful reports? (10:18)

11. In Jesus' prayer, for what does he praise God? (10:21)

12. How are Jesus' disciples blessed? (10:23-24)

13. What question prompts the telling of the parable of the good Samaritan? (10:25)

14. Who is "my neighbor"? (10:29, 36-37)

15. Who receives Jesus into her house? (10:38)

16. How does Mary upset Martha? (10:39-40)

Answer these questions by reading Luke 11:1-13

17. What is Luke's version of the Lord's Prayer? (11:2-4)

18. Why does the friend help his neighbor? (11:5-8)

19. In order to receive, what must one do? (11:10)

Answer these questions by reading Luke 11:14-28

20. When Jesus casts out a demon from a man who was mute, many are amazed. What do others say? (11:15)

21. What is Jesus' response? (11:17-20)

22. What happens when an evil spirit leaves a person? (11:24-26)

23. What reply does Jesus make to the woman who says, "Blessed is the mother who gave you birth and nursed you"? (11:27-28)

DIMENSION TWO:
WHAT DOES THE BIBLE MEAN?

In this lesson we begin a lengthy study of Jesus' journey from Galilee to Jerusalem by way of Samaria. Jesus sets his face to go to Jerusalem, his city of destiny. While on the journey, Jesus tries to prepare his disciples for the time when he will no longer be with them.

Jesus' teachings take a variety of forms—parables, wisdom sayings, proverbs, pronouncements, teachings, and miracle stories—in this lesson.

The Scripture is divided into five themes:

1. Conditions of Discipleship (9:51-62)
2. Mission of the Seventy-two (10:1-24)
3. Jesus Answers Questions (10:25-42)
4. Teachings About Prayer (11:1-13)
5. Casting Out Demons (11:14-28)

❑ *Luke 9:51-62.* These verses indicate Jesus' determination to go to Jerusalem for the Feast of the Passover. He "resolutely set out" toward the heart of religious leadership of Judaism, Jerusalem. Jesus is aware of what will happen to him, as it has happened to prophets before him: He will experience abuse, rejection, and death.

Jesus' immediate task is to train his disciples in the message of the good news of the kingdom of God. To prepare for his coming, Jesus sends disciples into a Samaritan village. Some people in the village reject his coming because Jesus is going through their land to Jerusalem.

James and John are furious at the Samaritans' rejection of Jesus. The question, "Lord, do you want us to call fire down from heaven to destroy them?" recalls an incident in the life of Elijah. Second Kings 1 records how the sick king Ahaziah sent messengers to the pagan god Baal-Zebub of the Philistines at Ekron to inquire about his health. Elijah met the messengers and sent them back to the king to tell him that he would die. The king then dispatched a captain and fifty men on three occasions. The first two sets were consumed by fire when Elijah shouted, "If I am a man of God, may fire come down from heaven and consume you and your fifty men!" (2 Kings 1:10, 12). The third captain begged Elijah for mercy.

Jesus realizes that his disciples do not understand his mission or the kingdom of God. After several years with Jesus, the disciples still looked for shows of dramatic power. Jesus did not come to coerce believers or to destroy those who refused his message. He came to call persons into the kingdom of God. The disciples must learn to love, not hate, those who oppose them. The disciples were to say to them, The kingdom of God is near you! These two fiery-minded fishermen had a lot to learn. Jesus now spends much of his time teaching the disciples.

In Luke 9:57-62, Jesus teaches the high cost of discipleship to three who want to follow him. Reread Questions 4, 5, and 6 in Dimension One from Jesus' perspective. Jesus has only a brief time before arriving in Jerusalem, facing possible death, and leaving the disciples untrained in so many areas. The conditions for discipleship require total giving of oneself—sacrificing personal security and intimacy of home life, minimizing filial duties, and even forgoing expressions of family affection. The times were tough for Jesus' last ministry to his disciples. They needed to be with him.

48

❏ *Luke 10:1-24.* Luke states that Jesus chooses seventy-two missioners (Other translations, including the NRSV, translate this as seventy. Jesus probably chooses seventy persons because the Book of Genesis lists seventy Gentile nations [Genesis 10]. The number *seventy* is often used by Bible writers to signify a large number. Thus, this choice of seventy disciples could symbolize the need to send missioners to all the nations of earth, that all persons may hear the good news of God's love and healing.) to go before him from Galilee to Jerusalem. Jesus sends his missioners out in groups of two.

The mission to the villages is successful, and all teams report with joy—noting especially how "even the demons submit to us in your name." Jesus suggests that they not rejoice about the demons they conquered; instead, he tells them "to rejoice that your names are written in heaven." Blind persons see; deaf persons hear; persons who were lame leap for joy; prisoners are set free. They know the kingdom of God has come into their lives. Jesus reminds these seventy-two disciples that their eyes are seeing what many prophets and kings have yearned to see and prayed to be a participant in—the ushering in of the kingdom of God.

❏ *Luke 10:25-37.* "An expert in the law" (the phrase used by Luke so his Gentile readers would understand the meaning of the word more commonly translated as "scribe") stands up and asks, "Teacher . . . what must I do to inherit eternal life?" [What must I do to be saved?] Jesus is aware that the questioner knows his Torah; so he asks, "What is written in the Law?" The expert in the law answers as expected, by reciting the verses from Deuteronomy 6:5 and Leviticus 19:18: " 'Love the Lord your God with all your heart and with all your soul and with all your strength and with all your mind'; and, 'Love your neighbor as yourself.' " Jesus replies, "You have answered correctly. Do this and you will live."

Now the expert in the law poses his real question: "And who is my neighbor?" To answer the expert in the law, Jesus tells a parable about a man who, on a journey, is robbed, beaten, and left "half dead." Two Jewish religious leaders come down the road, and neither offers the man assistance. Then a Samaritan sees the victim and immediately goes to him and binds up his wounds. The Samaritan puts him on his own beast, takes him to an inn, and cares for his financial needs. The Samaritan agrees to return later to pay any further bills. In light of the parable, who proves neighbor to the victim? The expert in the law pauses; he knows the answer but does not want to use the word *Samaritan*. So he replied, "The one who had mercy on him." Jesus says, "Go and do likewise."

In Luke the whole passage has a practical aim. Who is my neighbor? was a question of great concern to both first-century Judaism and the early church, and so it has a natural life situation in the ministry of Jesus and in the life of the early church. Jews and Samaritans hated one another at this time in history on religious and racial grounds. Therefore, the purpose of the parable is to give a practical example of neighborliness to teach love of neighbor. Loving God finds practical proof in the love of neighbors, and loving neighbors receives its foundation from the love of God. It is on the foundation of this love for God that the love of the neighbor is built up. The love of the neighbor aims at helping anyone in need simply because the person is a fellow human being.

❏ *Luke 10:38-42.* In contrast to the good Samaritan, who was a doer of the Word, Mary emphasizes the intangible aspect of faith. While Martha is busy "doing" the meal, Mary (in the attitude of a pupil) sits at Jesus' feet. She listens, probably asking occasional questions. Jesus has been living in various homes, teaching his followers the meaning of discipleship, and is undoubtedly not at rest about his future in Jerusalem. Jesus needs a friend who will listen to and talk with him. Mary is that friend. Martha wants to be kind too—in her own way, which means preparing a good meal. Mary meets Jesus' real needs, and Martha misses participating in his messianic feast of words.

❏ *Luke 11:1-13.* Another question arises: How should we pray? Jesus says, First address God as Father. The word *Father* includes the emotional overtones of respect, affection, and love. Then, hallow his name. Ezekiel weeps with the heartbroken deity who tells how his people's conduct "wherever they went among the nations . . . profaned my holy name" (Ezekiel 36:20). People who have faith in the Lord must reflect the nature and character of the God they worship—and in so doing, they hallow his holy name. In hallowing his name, we give the kingdom of God primary place in life. "Your kingdom come" presupposes our basic desire to see God's will prevail in all areas of our lives. When we ask God to "give us each day our daily bread," we simply ask that he supply our needs. "Lead us not into temptation" requests that we not be subject to trials or temptations so severe that they undermine our loyalty to his purposes.

❑ *Luke 11:14-28.* In New Testament times, medical doctors knew nothing of germs and bacteria or of psychosomatic medicine. So Dr. Luke, following the learning of his day, ascribed dumbness, deafness, blindness, epilepsy, and various other illnesses to demon possession. Jesus rightly taught that these maladies are not the will of God, whose will is health and wholeness of the entire person. Jesus brought healing to many people. All of us need the cleansing touch of his Spirit upon our lives.

DIMENSION THREE:
WHAT DOES THE BIBLE MEAN TO ME?

Prayer Life

Perhaps the most important practice in a Christian's life is his or her prayer life. What and how a Christian prays is more important than where and when. The Lord's Prayer says nothing about the acceptable length of prayers. In fact, Jesus' prayer is quite brief, succinctly stating what he wants God to respond to in our daily lives or experiences. Nor does Jesus establish a particular time of day for prayer; it depends on the person.

But Jesus does consider that what we ask of God is important. As with Ezekiel, some actions (and even prayers) profane God's name. Some Christians, as do some Jews, do not hallow, but profane, God's name by actions and purposes that are immoral and contrary to God's dreams for us. We profane God's name when we ask God to do that which lacks mercy, supports injustice, encourages greed, and substitutes lust for love.

JESUS SETS HIS FACE TOWARD JERUSALEM **51**

Jesus assumes God knows all things—God is omniscient. Yet God's omniscience should not keep us from asking and knocking. Some things come only by our asking. Asking may be a way of saying, "Father, I know you need my energies to support your concerns. Here are my energies; please use them." Also, true petitionary prayer (asking and knocking) is an act of exploration—exploring the breadth and depth of the mind of God in order to discover the divine will. Prayer is often a time of hard work.

Martha and Mary's experience with Jesus can challenge us to ask the right questions. Martha wants to do the kindest thing she can for Jesus. Her sin of omission is to consider, not what Jesus wants and needs most, but what she wants for him and needs most for herself. Mary listens to Jesus' heart—his yearnings, attitudes, and hopes. Martha listens to his stomach. Both women were right, though Mary chose what was "better."

You also must be ready, because the Son of Man
will come at an hour when you do not expect him (12:40).

— 7 —

True Discipleship
and Its Opponents
Luke 11:29–13:9

DIMENSION ONE:
WHAT DOES THE BIBLE SAY?

Answer these questions by reading Luke 11:29-36

1. What sign will this generation receive? (11:29)

2. Jesus says that he embodies something greater than the talents of two great biblical persons. Who are they, and what are their talents? (11:31-32)

3. After lighting a lamp, where does one put it, and why? (11:33)

4. What serves to light the body, and how does it function? (11:34)

5. When Jesus dines with a Pharisee, what astonishes the Pharisee? (11:37-38)

6. What does Jesus call the Pharisee? (11:40)

7. What does Jesus condemn in his three "woes" to the Pharisees? (11:42-44)

8. What does Jesus condemn in his three "woes" to the experts in the law? (11:46-47, 52)

9. What does Jesus first say to the thousands who gather to hear him? (12:1)

Answer these questions by reading Luke 12:2-48

10. What does Jesus say to those followers who may and will face persecution? (12:4)

11. What is the unforgivable sin? (12:10)

12. What is more important than food and clothing? (12:23)

13. Why is it important that one invest in "a treasure in heaven that will not be exhausted"? (12:33-34)

14. In what condition does the master expect to find his servants? (12:36-37a)

15. What does the master do when he comes home? (12:37b)

16. What is the key to the demands the master places upon his various servants? (12:48b)

Answer these questions by reading Luke 12:49–13:9

17. According to Jesus, does he come to bring peace or division? (12:51)

18. How will a family experience this division? (12:53)

19. Why should persons attempt to settle their differences out of court? (12:57-58)

20. What question does Jesus ask in order to turn a political issue (Pilate's slaying of several Galileans in the Temple) into a religious issue? (13:2)

21. What is Jesus' response to this religious issue? (13:3)

22. What advice does the man give the person who took care of the vineyard about the fruitless fig tree? (13:8-9)

DIMENSION TWO:
WHAT DOES THE BIBLE MEAN?

The Scripture for this lesson is divided into four themes:

1. The Sign of Jonah and Two Parables (11:29-36)
2. Denunciation of Pharisees and Lawyers (11:37–12:1)
3. Responsibilities of Discipleship (12:2-48)
4. Reflections on Christ's Ministry (12:49–13:9)

❑ *Luke 11:29-36.* "As the crowds increased, Jesus said, 'This is a wicked generation. It asks for a miraculous sign, but none will be given it except the sign of Jonah' " (11:29).

The Ninevites never asked Jonah for a sign, for these pagan disbelievers did not need a sign. They accepted the message of Jonah and were immediately converted. But many Jews who believed in God asked Jesus for a sign about himself. Jesus commented that when the Queen of Sheba rises on the Day of Judgment, she will condemn them for spiritual blindness; for something "greater than Solomon . . . [and] Jonah is here," namely, the Messiah. But they refuse to see.

However, keep in mind that though Jesus heals the sick, at the same time he always asks those he heals not to tell others who healed them. Jesus' admonition is part of the "messianic secret." Jesus does reveal himself as the Messiah to the Twelve, but only when they themselves recognize him as such—as at the Mount of Transfiguration and at Caesarea Philippi. Jesus' temptations in the wilderness explain his concern for secrecy. His primary mission and goal is to preach and teach the presence of the Kingdom and to win converts to God and God's kingdom.

Perhaps Luke 11:33-36 has a bigger interpretation than is generally given. The Scripture may well mean that Jesus is the lamp that ought to be judiciously set in places where his light can illuminate the darkness of our emptiness, hopelessness, and despair. We need the light from the lamp of God to shine in those damp and dark areas of our lives where demonic attitudes and purposes would destroy us and our friends and indeed the world.

❑ *Luke 11:37–12:1.* Jesus accepts an invitation to have a meal with a Pharisee. At the table, the host notices his guest (Jesus) has not washed his hands. This lack of ritual cleansing was considered a sin, breaking one of the hundreds of oral rules. These rules were unwritten (that is, oral) interpretations and applications of the Mosaic law. The written laws were in the Torah. The unwritten laws were memorized by experts in the law and passed from generation to generation. The experts in the law were the learned men of the law, and they gave instructions in the law by way of the synagogue. They had the care of the law. And their duty was to make transcripts of it.

The experts in the law developed scores of applications of the unwritten laws for each of the Ten Commandments. A person could break the sabbath in 613 different ways. The basic rule is that a person shall do no work on the sabbath (Exodus 20:8-11). But what is work? During the four centuries before the Christian era, the elders defined work under thirty-nine categories. Each category was subdivided into literally thousands of rules and regulations. To illustrate, one of the categories under *work* is "burden." But what is a "burden"? The elders made the meaning clear: "A burden is food equal in weight to a dried fig . . . milk enough to moisten an eye-salve, paper enough to write a custom-house notice upon, ink enough to write two letters. . . . A tailor breaks the Sabbath if he forgets and leaves a needle under his robe." (See *The Gospel of Matthew*, Vol. 1, by William Barclay; Westminster Press, 1975; page 128.) Thus sin is clearly defined and understood by the Pharisees who tried to live under the law of the experts in the law. Morality was not defined in terms of prophetic words like *justice, mercy,* and *compassion.* Jesus is furious at religious leaders who subvert high ethical demands for cheap discipleship.

Jesus says, "Woe to you Pharisees" who are meticulous in obeying the unwritten laws. You should also be meticulous in obeying the written law of justice and love. But you do not! Jesus addresses the second woe to Pharisees who love to sit in the front seats of the synagogue and be greeted with deference and exaggerated salutation. Such actions were hardly expressions of the will and purpose of God. The third woe refers to the consequences of their dedication to observing the minutia of the oral laws: They have overlooked the weightier matters of the law—a life of moral action, justice, and love. The Pharisees' misplacement of true values has a terrible effect on others. Pharisees mislead those who honor them; they "are like unmarked graves, which men walk over without knowing it."

Jesus then turns to the experts in the law. Woe to you "because you load people down with burdens they can hardly carry, and you yourselves will not lift one finger to help them" (11:46). The second woe refers to their nonsupport of present prophets (such as himself). They spend their time building tombs and monuments for those who were martyred years ago. The third woe expresses Jesus' sorrow at the consequences of their scribal labors: The "burdens" of their thousands of rules has an effect of taking away the key to knowledge.

❑ *Luke 12:2-48.* As Jesus speaks to his disciples, perhaps they recall the power of yeast to change the character of bread. It takes only a small amount of yeast to change a whole loaf. Only small amounts of the yeast of legalism, externalism, pious ostentation, and pride in one's spiritual achievements are required to transform an otherwise good person into a religious hypocrite.

Jesus urges his disciples to fear this leaven of hypocrisy; for it will kill the human spirit, making them candidates for hell (12:1-5). Jesus asks for loyalty and trust, even when persecuted for his sake. God still loves and is present with them when all else seems to fail. Jesus asks them never to blaspheme the Holy Spirit. This sin is unforgivable (12:10).

In the parable of the rich fool (12:13-21), Jesus portrays a man dedicated to nothing more than gaining possessions. He has gathered only physical things and has gained no treasures in the kingdom of God. He is poverty-stricken when it comes to the jewels of the spirit.

❑ *Luke 12:49–13:9.* Jesus asks, "Do you think I came to bring peace on earth?" His answer is, No, rather division within families, who will often dislike having a son or daughter or mother or father following his ways. But everyone must make a decision regardless of divisions. Loyalty to God's way of life as seen in Jesus must take precedence over other loyalties if life is to reflect kinship with God.

Jesus turns to a political issue (concerning Pilate's alleged murder of some Galileans). Jesus asks, Did these men die because God willed it? Were they worse sinners than others in Jerusalem? No! They died because no one called their attention to the danger about them. "Unless you repent, you too will all perish." Look out; beware of that which can destroy your spirit. Choose now the way to life. (See Luke 13:1-9.)

DIMENSION THREE:
WHAT DOES THE BIBLE MEAN TO ME?

"Knowing" and the Law

The Pharisees and experts in the law were of vital concern to Jesus, who knew many of these people personally and loved them. But he was concerned about the effects of their "rule-religion" on their lives and on those they affected by their practices. He also valued the abilities and dedication of the experts in the law (who formed the core of Pharisaism), but he yearned to lift them beyond the minutia of their legalism.

Jesus says the experts in the law are responsible for taking away "the key of knowledge" (11:52). We think of the great prophet Hosea who declared, "My people are destroyed from lack of knowledge" (Hosea 4:6). Hosea was describing the priesthood of his day. The priests were the instructors in the law of his time. Hosea charged the priests on two accounts: (1) They were too content to receive their share of the sacrifices at the expense of not informing people as to the nature of God. (2) The priests emphasized knowing about God rather than knowing God personally.

Both charges were valid in Jesus' time and still apply to some religious people today. Jesus knew that many pious Jews were replacing a personal walk with God with obedience to thousands of rules. Little wonder that Jesus said, "Come to me, all you who are weary and burdened [burdened with rule-religion], and I will give you rest" (Matthew 11:28). Persons who try to fulfill the minutia of the law have no rest—either then or now.

*Make every effort to enter through the narrow door,
because many, I tell you, will try to enter and
will not be able to (13:24).*

8

The Life of Discipleship
Luke 13:10–15:32

DIMENSION ONE:
WHAT DOES THE BIBLE SAY?

Answer these questions by reading Luke 13:10-35

1. Where is Jesus when he cures a woman? (13:10-13)

2. Why is the ruler of the synagogue upset? (13:14)

3. What does the ruler say to the people? (13:14)

4. In essence, what does Jesus say to the ruler? (13:15-16)

5. Jesus compares the kingdom of God with what two things?
   (13:18-21)

6. When someone asks how many will be saved (13:23), what is Jesus' reply? (13:24-30)

7. When some Pharisees tell Jesus he should "leave this place and go somewhere else" because Herod wants to kill him, what does Jesus say? (13:31-33)

8. After Jesus laments over Jerusalem, when does he hint he will be there? (13:35b)

Answer these questions by reading Luke 14

9. One sabbath while dining with a ruler of the synagogue, what does Jesus do? (14:1-6)

10. What is Jesus' main point in the parable on choosing a seat at the wedding feast? (14:11)

11. Whom does Jesus recommend you invite to a feast? (14:12-13)

12. Why will you be blessed for inviting these people? (14:14)

13. What excuses do people make who are invited to a great banquet? (14:18-20)

14. In anger the master tells his servant to go out and get some guests. Whom does he say to get? (14:21-23)

15. What four challenges does Jesus give to those who want to be his disciples? (14:26-35)

16. To whom does Jesus say, "He who has ears to hear, let him hear"? (14:25, 35)

Answer these questions by reading Luke 15

17. What is the cause of the muttering of the Pharisees and the teachers of the law? (15:2)

18. Where does the shepherd who loses a sheep leave his ninety-nine other sheep while searching for the lost one? (15:4)

19. As a woman and her friends will rejoice in her finding a lost silver coin, who will rejoice over one sinner who repents? (15:10)

20. What is the major sign of the younger son's degradation? (15:15-16)

21. What does the younger son think his relationship to his father is? (15:19)

22. How does the father receive his lost son? (15:20-24)

23. How does the elder son react to the younger son's return? (15:25-30)

DIMENSION TWO:
WHAT DOES THE BIBLE MEAN?

The Scripture for this lesson, "The Life of Discipleship," is divided into five themes:

1. Sabbath and God's New Creation (13:10-21)
2. Teachings During the Journey (13:22-35)
3. Table Talk in the House of a Pharisee (14:1-24)
4. The Conditions of Discipleship (14:25-35)
5. God's Love for the Lost (15:1-32)

❑ *Luke 13:10-21.* The healing of a woman who has had a spinal weakness for eighteen years occurs in a synagogue. Several significant things take place:

(1) This event is Luke's last account of Jesus being present in a synagogue. Jesus teaches several times in the homes of Pharisees after this occasion, but not in their synagogues.

(2) While Jesus is teaching in a synagogue on the sabbath, he sees a woman who is "bent over and could not straighten up at all" (13:11). Jesus calls to her—an unheard of practice. Rabbis (teachers) did not teach women, nor were women permitted to go beyond the latticework in the back of the synagogue. That is why we never hear of a Jewish woman asking Jesus for help except in Matthew 20:20 and John 11:20-22. But Jesus calls her, and she comes to where he is teaching.

(3) Jesus lays his hands on the woman and pronounces her healed. The woman praises God. The Pharisees and experts in the law are horrified because Jesus is "working" on the sabbath, which violates many of the Jewish laws. This violation of the sabbath upsets the ruler of the synagogue. After all, Jesus, who was cleared and even invited to teach by the ruler, has willfully broken many of the sabbath laws. Standing up, the ruler faces his congregation and speaks with righteous indignation: "There are six days for work. So come and be healed on those days, not on the Sabbath" (13:14). Jesus says, "You hypocrites!" Jesus then accuses those present by reminding them that on the sabbath they untie their oxen or donkeys and lead them to water. Ought not this daughter of Abraham be loosed from her bonds, too?—and especially so on the Lord's day, for the Lord has healed her. Do not be angry; be grateful and thank God! "When he had said this, all his opponents were humiliated; but the people were delighted with all the wonderful things he [Jesus] was doing" (13:17).

Jesus then describes what the kingdom of God is like. Jesus says the Kingdom is like a grain of mustard seed and like leaven. This twofold reference means the Kingdom has small beginnings (as is the case with the extremely small mustard seed and with leaven). Yet both multiply themselves until one can offer nesting to many birds and the other can multiply an amount of bread.

❏ *Luke 13:22-35.* In Luke 13:22-30 Jesus admits that the number to be saved will be few, for the door is narrow. Some who are outside the door say that they ate and drank in his presence and that he even taught them in the streets. Apparently they were not apt disciples, for Jesus saw no spark of excitement in their eyes as he spoke to them. The assumption that they will be saved because they are descendants of Abraham and Isaac and Jacob is irrelevant. For, as the opening chapter of the Gospel of John (1:1-18) says, it is not by flesh and blood (genes and chromosomes) that a person enters the kingdom of God, but by the grace of God.

❏ *Luke 14:1-24.* Luke's report of Jesus' third time in the home of a ruler of the synagogue is full of suspicion and intrigue. The experts in the law (also called scribes) and the Pharisees are watching him "carefully" to see if they can catch him doing something he should not do. And Jesus obliges them by healing a man who has dropsy (edema—swollen, with too much water in his body). Jesus says something like this, "If you have a son or an ox that has fallen into a well or cistern on the sabbath, would not every one of you save the life of the son or ox by pulling it out of the water? How much more a man who is drowning in his bodily fluids (edema)? Would you not set him free from death by drowning, too?" No one can reply.

At the dinner, Jesus tells a parable (14:7-14) about a self-admiring man who comes to a dinner party and chooses a place of honor for himself near the host. Later, the host brings a dignitary who is seated next to the host. Thus the self-admiring man is forced to forfeit his good seat, and (with all good seats now taken) he goes to an unworthy seat at the edges of the party. "For everyone who exalts himself will be humbled, and he who humbles himself will be exalted" (14:11). Jesus says that when you give a feast, do not invite your relatives and friends, even though you have good fellowship in kindred minds. Instead, invite the deaf, speechless, maimed, blind, and poor so they will have a chance to be edified in spiritual matters. Your recompense will be to see them in heaven because of your thoughtfulness and kindness.

Another parable Jesus tells is about "a great banquet" (perhaps the messianic banquet?). The invitations are issued, the time arrives, and so do the excuses. One man has just bought a new field. Another has just bought a fine five-yoke team of oxen. A third man has recently married and therefore asks to be excused from attending the big banquet. The persons with invitations represent the Pharisees and experts in the law. They now lose their opportunity to be at the table. Instead, servants go out to get two groups: Jewish sinners ("the poor, the crippled, the blind and the lame") and Gentiles. These lower classes will become the higher classes because of those with whom they now associate. They accept the invitation to the banquet.

❑ *Luke 14:25-35.* One of four conditions for a would-be disciple is to "hate his father and mother, his wife and children, his brothers and sisters—yes, even his own life." The verb *miseo* (hate) is a Greek word that is not intended to be taken literally. It means "to love less than" or "to postpone in love." Jesus says that those who love him less than they love their father, mother, sister, or brother are unworthy to become his disciples. This demand to have no greater love than love for Christ leads to three other conditions of discipleship: (1) Each disciple is expected to bear his or her cross. (2) Each disciple must take time to analyze himself or herself to see if he or she can make it. (3) Each disciple must be a person of salty qualities: giving zest, flavor, and a redemptive touch to those around him or her.

❑ *Luke 15:1-32.* Luke combines several parables whose themes focus on one major point: how persons become "lost." Jesus' parables suggest four ways of becoming lost: (1) like a sheep—by folly; (2) like a silver coin—by carelessness; (3) like the young man—by willfully choosing the way of "wild living"; and (4) like the elder brother—by jealousy, hurt pride, and arrogance.

Let us take these ways one at a time to see what they mean. The parable of the lost sheep and the good shepherd (15:4-7) has roots in Ezekiel 34:11-16 and Isaiah 40:11. Jesus assumes that everyone would be compassionate and go, without a further thought, to save the lost sheep. Finding the sheep, the shepherd's rejoicing is multiplied by that of his friends and neighbors who understand his feelings. So Jesus says, "There will be more rejoicing in heaven over one sinner who repents than over ninety-nine righteous persons who do not need to repent" (15:7).

THE LIFE OF DISCIPLESHIP

The same joy and trust in God as a caring and loving God is told in the next parable—which has a similar point—about a woman who loses one of her ten silver coins. As the first parable tells of a man who lost a sheep, this parable tells of a woman who loses a precious coin. But each item is lost in a different way. The sheep nibbled itself into the wilderness, not being aware of where it was going, which is the folly of many persons too. They get lost without thinking where their paths are taking them. The woman apparently loses her coin through carelessness.

The prodigal son becomes lost as he willfully follows his immoral choices in the far country. Finally, he is living with pigs as a pig. He eventually "came to his senses" and let his memory play on his father's house and attitudes. The son rises from the level of an animal's existence to that of a thinking, choosing man. He goes home and is welcomed by his father, not as a servant, but as a son. His father loves him, dresses him as his son, and prepares a banquet for him who was dead and is alive, who was lost and is found. So God, Jesus teaches, loves and yearns for his lost ones.

The elder son has wrapped himself in a cocoon of self-righteous pride and self-pity and is smothering in his hate and unbrotherly attitudes. He says in effect, "Father, this son of yours has squandered your living." The father replies, "Son, your brother is alive and well. Rejoice." With boundless love, God yearns for those who are lost by folly; by carelessness; by willful intentions to see the far country; and by the poisons of hate, selfishness, and undisciplined passions. Though all were lost, all need not be lost.

DIMENSION THREE:
WHAT DOES THE BIBLE MEAN TO ME?

Luke 15—Jesus and the Lost

In Luke 15 Jesus speaks to the tax collectors and sinners. But the Pharisees and the experts in the law are not happy. They murmur and are filled with indignation. The reason for their murmuring is, "This man welcomes sinners and eats with them." Jesus accepts their words as true and tells the parables in Luke 15. These parables are united into a connected story by the word *lost.* Consider Luke 15:1-32 in Dimension Two. In your opinion who are the lost? Are the lost like a sheep who has strayed away from the shepherd and away from the flock? Are the lost like a silver coin that renders no service because of being out of circulation? Are the lost like the prodigal son who is not at home with his father? who is not creating and is destroying? In what sense is the decent, earnest, and hard-working elder son lost?

Whoever can be trusted with very little can also be trusted with much, and whoever is dishonest with very little will also be dishonest with much (16:10).

—— **9** ——

The Use and Abuse of Wealth
Luke 16–17

DIMENSION ONE:
WHAT DOES THE BIBLE SAY?

Answer these questions by reading Luke 16

1. To whom does Jesus tell the parable about a rich man who employs a dishonest manager? (16:1)

2. What is the manager accused of doing? (16:1)

3. On confronting his manager, what does the rich man order him to do? (16:2)

4. Why does the scheming manager call in his master's debtors and discount their bills? (16:4)

5. For what does the master commend the manager? (16:8)

6. If a person is dishonest in a very little, what might one expect of that person in a larger capacity? (16:10)

7. Into what two periods does Jesus divide time? (16:16)

8. Who lies at the rich man's gate? (16:19-20)

9. What happens when Lazarus dies? (16:22a)

10. What happens when the rich man dies? (16:22b-23)

11. To whom does the rich man want Abraham to send Lazarus, and why? (16:27-28)

12. What is Abraham's response to the rich man? (16:31)

Answer the following questions by reading Luke 17

13. What does Jesus say about the sin of causing others to sin? (17:2)

14. If a brother sins against you seven times in the day and turns to you seven times and says, "I repent," what must you do? (17:4)

15. How do the disciples reply? (17:5)

16. Why does one not thank a servant who does what he or she is told to do? (17:9-10)

17. As Jesus enters a village, he meets ten persons who had leprosy who ask for mercy. What does he tell them? (17:14)

18. As the persons who had leprosy go by, they are cleansed. Why does one person who had leprosy return and fall at Jesus' feet? (17:15-16)

19. Which one of the ten persons who had leprosy thanks Jesus? (17:16-18)

20. What does Jesus say to Pharisees who ask when the kingdom of God is coming? (17:20-21)

21. What warning does Jesus give his disciples about the false teachers who say the Kingdom is here, or the Kingdom is there? (17:22-23)

22. What lesson can one learn from "the days of Noah" and "the days of Lot" with regard to "the day the Son of Man is revealed"? (17:33)

DIMENSION TWO:
WHAT DOES THE BIBLE MEAN?

The Scripture for this lesson is divided into four themes:

1. Faithfulness in Administration (16:1-15)
2. The Gospel and Wealth (16:16-31)
3. Forgiveness, Faith, Grace, and Ingratitude (17:1-19)
4. The Kingdom of God (17:20-37)

❑ *Luke 16:1-15.* The opening parable of the shrewd (or dishonest) manager is one of the more difficult of Jesus' stories to interpret. Jesus had firm attitudes toward virtues such as honesty, justice, and mercy. His teachings would not violate these significant goals in human living. We need to keep this teaching in mind as we ask what Jesus means when he commends the shrewd, but dishonest, manager.

Jesus is speaking, not to the crowd, but to his disciples (which is a larger number than the Twelve). His concern is to emphasize the importance of being mentally quick and alert. So Jesus tells a parable about a rich man who owns several farms, with an overall manager (steward). The rich man hears reports that his manager is "wasting his [the owner's] possessions." The owner calls the manager in to face the charges against him. Apparently, the charges are true and his actions well-known; for the manager does not deny the charges. The owner tells the manager to get his records for each farm and to bring them to him, after which the manager is fired.

Returning to his home, the manager's mind is quick and scheming. He faces unemployment. He must come up with a plan that will make the renters of each farm morally, if not economically, indebted to him. He takes wise, though not moral, thought before acting and draws up the following plan: Before his renters find out he is to be fired, he will call them to an immediate accounting of what they owe him (and thus the master). He orders them to appear, one at a time. Notice that payments are made, not in money, but in kind—that is, the wheat farmer pays a percentage of his produce to the owner; the man who owns an olive orchard pays a percentage of olive oil. The manager asks his first renter, "How much do you owe my master?" He replies, "Eight hundred gallons of olive oil." And the manager says to the renter, "Take your bill, sit down quickly, and make it four hundred." The manager reduces his bill by half. The second farmer, who has his acreage in wheat, says he owes a thousand bushels of wheat. The scheming manager prudently reduces it to eight hundred, gaining the renter's gratitude. The renters apparently are unaware of the dishonesty behind the reduction in the amount due; they assume generosity by the master.

When the master hears the scheme, he admires the alert mind of his manager and commends him for his shrewdness. He certainly could not approve of the manager's dishonesty— it had cost the master dearly. But the manager placed him in a dilemma. If he calls the various renters together and tells them of the fraud, he admits that he has been outwitted by a manager. Worse yet, by now the renters are thanking him for his generosity, kindness, and concern for their needs. Dare he turn down such a good reputation?

Jesus applauds and commends the alert mind that is capable of creative action and decision. Jesus suggests that his disciples develop such alertness for deciding and acting on matters of the kingdom of God. Let the "people of the light" be as shrewd as the "people of this world." The real point of this parable is the act of God. The kingdom of God is a different world as compared with all that is earthly, and the kingdom of God is a gift of the grace and love of God.

❑ *Luke 16:16-31.* Jesus says, "Everyone is forcing his way into [the kingdom of God]." When a person makes a decision for the Kingdom, he or she has many decisions to make, some requiring sweat and tears before making final covenants. Rebirth is often violent, as is the continual struggle to live out the Kingdom.

The theme of this section, "The Gospel and Wealth," comes from another of Jesus' parables: the rich man and Lazarus. In Old Testament times, the place of the dead was called Sheol. At death all persons went to Sheol, to one of the two sections of Sheol: Paradise, for those who were moral and religious prior to death, and Gehenna, or hell, for those who were immoral and irreligious. The story of the rich man and Lazarus presupposes this idea of life after death. A great chasm, or divide, separated the two areas; those in each place could not visit one another, but they could see and hear one another.

The rich man probably is a Sadducee, who did not believe in life after death. He is well dressed and feasts sumptuously every day. Lazarus, on the other hand, is poor and sick (He lay at the gate of the rich man.).

Lazarus dies and "the angels carr[y] him to Abraham's side." The rich man dies and is buried; and his spirit goes, not to Paradise, but to hell (or Hades). Here he suffers torment, especially lack of a cool drink. He requests that Abraham send Lazarus to quench his thirst. Abraham refuses. The rich man then asks Abraham to send Lazarus to his father's house to warn his five brothers about the evil consequences of selfish and thoughtless living at the expense of the poor. Abraham denies this request, too. No one would believe Lazarus's message. "If they do not listen to Moses and the Prophets, they will not be convinced even if someone rises from the dead."

❑ *Luke 17:1-19.* Jesus expresses strong feelings when he thinks of persons who willfully mislead the newborn Christian. He says it is better "for [them] to be thrown into the sea with a millstone tied around [their] neck" (17:2). On the other hand, disciples are to take an affirmative stand and lovingly rebuke those persons who mislead others by their messages or their immoral lives (17:3). Yet amazingly, the disciples are to forgive just such persons, not once, but seven times a day or whatever number of times a person repents (17:4).

In Luke 17:7-10, the parable of the servant reminds us that we are to live dutiful lives that express our gratitude to God. Some things—expressions of trust and hope, actions of justice and love, thoughts of concern for the hungry—we do automatically. Many of our spontaneous thoughts and actions stem from the nature of our lives in God's kingdom.

The healing of the persons who had leprosy in 17:11-19 expresses Jesus' concern for ingratitude. Ten persons who had leprosy were healed by Jesus; but only one (a Samaritan) returned, rejoicing and praising God for what Jesus did for him.

DIMENSION THREE:
WHAT DOES THE BIBLE MEAN TO ME?

Luke 16:19-31—The Gospel and Hell

The parable of the rich man and Lazarus makes us ponder about Sheol, with its two divisions of Paradise and Gehenna (hell). While on the cross, Jesus said to a fellow sufferer, "Today you will be with me in paradise" (Luke 23:43). A second man, one of the criminals, railed at him, saying, "Aren't you the Christ? Save yourself and us!" (Luke 23:39). How Jesus was hurt by the criminal's verbal barbs—making light of his being the Messiah, the reason he was on the cross.

I recall the look on the face of a fine and dedicated chaplain as he returned from seeing Auschwitz. He was physically torn asunder by what he saw. After sitting for some time, he finally said, "Horace, there must be a hell! The tortures, pain, unbelievable inhumanity, must be faced by those who perpetrated these horrible tragedies. They must see and feel the consequences of their evil decisions." Perhaps part of Sheol includes facing up to what our choices have done to others, as well as to ourselves. What did the rich man's selfish gluttony do to Lazarus's family and those who loved him and suffered with him? Perhaps the rich man needs to know. On the other hand, what might paradise be like? Is it a time for reviewing old memories and perhaps developing a reservoir of new and marvelous memories of current experiences with Christ?

In 17:21, Jesus says, "The kingdom of God is within you." Take time to look. Also, is it not true that for many of us the kingdom of hell is in our midst—within us and among us? Dare we look? Aware of the pain of our drug culture, the horrors of child and spouse abuse, the haunted look of millions of hungry people as they move through starvation to death, what message do we have for those trapped in the kingdom of hell? If the Bible means anything to us, what must we do to help those who live in paradise "descend" into the kingdom of hell to bring good news?

Luke 17:11-19—Gratitude and Ingratitude

The story of the ten persons who had leprosy is a parable about gratitude and ingratitude. Ninety percent of those healed of leprosy were too busy going to Jerusalem to take time to thank their healer. They had been set free of a loathsome disease. They had lived in hovels. They were in pain, cold, hungry, unwanted—feared. Now they are free to go about doing what they had done before they contracted this terrible ailment. We wonder if their lives were really changed, other than having a dread disease healed. Were they really whole? Had they experienced the wholeness that Jesus gave—not only peace of mind, but wholeness throughout their entire body, mind, and soul?

Only the Samaritan, the foreigner, the Gentile, broke the record of ingratitude. He came and fell at Jesus' feet, praising God. Free at last. Thank God, I'm free!

What is impossible with men is possible with God (18:27).

— 10 —
The Kingdom of God
Luke 18:1–19:44

DIMENSION ONE:
WHAT DOES THE BIBLE SAY?

Answer these questions by reading Luke 18

1. In the parable of the unjust judge, how often does Jesus say they should pray? (18:1)

2. What does the widow ask the judge to do? (18:3)

3. What word does Jesus use to describe the judge? (18:6)

4. Who are the two men who go into the Temple to pray? (18:10)

5. In his prayer, what kinds of people does the Pharisee say he is not like? (18:11)

6. What does the Pharisee do? (18:12)

7. How does the tax collector pray? (18:13)

8. What does he ask God in his prayer? (18:13)

9. What does Jesus say when the people bring infants to him? (18:16)

10. What does the ruler lack to inherit eternal life? (18:22)

11. How does Jesus answer the question "Who then can be saved"? (18:27)

12. What will happen to Jesus? (18:32-33)

13. What does Jesus say to the blind man when he asks to have his sight restored? (18:42)

14. Who tries to see Jesus in Jericho? (19:2-3)

15. What does he do so he can see Jesus? (19:4)

16. What does Jesus say to Zacchaeus when he says he will give half of his possessions to the poor? (19:9)

17. What happens to the person who does not put the money in the bank to collect interest? (19:23-24)

18. What does Jesus ask two disciples to do at Bethphage? (19:30)

19. What are they to say when someone asks them about taking the colt? (19:31)

20. What does the crowd of disciples say as Jesus rides the colt down the Mount of Olives? (19:38)

21. What does Jesus predict about Jerusalem? (19:44)

DIMENSION TWO:
WHAT DOES THE BIBLE MEAN?

The Scripture for this lesson is divided into four themes:

1. Parables on the Practice of Prayer (18:1-14)
2. Conditions of Entrance to the Kingdom (18:15-34)
3. Jesus in Jericho (18:35–19:27)
4. Jesus' Ministry in Jerusalem (19:28-44)

❏ *Luke 18:1-14.* Jesus tells his disciples a parable about the practice of prayer. There was a judge "who neither feared God nor cared about [paid no attention to] men"—he did as he pleased. He had no moral scruples about giving or denying justice.

A widow wants the judge to grant her justice, to clear her of suspicion, dishonor, or a charge of wrongdoing. For example, the widow may own a lawn mower; and an enemy may suspect that she stole it. After all, a poor widow cannot afford one; and he had heard that a friend of his had his lawn mower stolen a year ago. That makes one wonder about the widow's honesty, doesn't it? The widow needs to be cleared (vindicated) because her friends and neighbors are talking about her and watching her carefully lest she steal something from them. The widow persists in her requests to the judge to grant her justice. Finally, he says, "She's wearing me out; I'll vindicate her."

Now, does Jesus want us to compare God with the immoral judge and conclude that as persistence moved the judge to action, so God will hear our pleas if we only annoy God enough? What does our answer to this question say about the character of God? Is God like that? Of course not! So, we ask, How else does Jesus use parables besides comparing God with some person or thing? The answer is "contrast." This parable of the judge and the widow suggests that we contrast the moral and loving God with the immoral and self-centered judge. When we do that, we find ourselves saying, If a mean judge gives in to persistent requests because of annoyance, how much more will a loving God respond to requests of those who ask him for understanding and help. God wants to help.

THE KINGDOM OF GOD   **81**

In the second parable, Luke 18:9-14, Jesus analyzes prayer from two perspectives—that of a sinner who repents and that of sons of Abraham "who were confident of their own righteousness." Two men go to the Temple to pray. One is a Pharisee, the other a publican (a despicable Jewish tax collector for Rome). The Pharisee stands in a conspicuous place and "pray[s] about himself [not to God]." His prayer catalogues the vices of persons who made no attempt to obey the letter of the oral or written law. They were "robbers, evildoers, adulterers." He boasts that he fasts twice a week and tithes, not only of the produce of the farms but also of everything he gets. He is so religious and pious, God must almost bow down to his piety and pray to him.

Contrast the Pharisee's prayer life with that of the loathed tax collector, who stands far from the altar. He is so contrite that he beats his breast and asks God for mercy. Jesus says that it is the tax collector who returns home justified—with a wonderful feeling of having been given an opportunity for a new start in life. The parable asks us to look at our prayer habits—both our words and our personal idiosyncrasies as we pray to God. What does our spiritual attitude say about prayer?

❏ *Luke 18:15-34.* Jesus illustrates the first condition for entering the kingdom of God as he takes infants in his arms and blesses them. They are so trusting, open to suggestions, and ready to try new things—of such is the Kingdom made. Persons who refuse to be childlike (not childish) do not meet the entrance requirements.

The parable of the rich ruler illustrates the second condition for entering the kingdom of God. Things can so dominate and control our thinking and actions that they become barriers to wholehearted devotion to the cause of Christ and his kingdom. Persons who value possessions in life are not fit to be followers of Jesus Christ. The rich ruler had diligently obeyed the laws. He thought he needed nothing more and was sad when he heard Jesus say that in his case he must rid himself of that which possessed him. Only then could he be free to be a follower in the fullest sense of the word. Though rich in things of the earth, he was poverty-stricken in the treasures of heaven. He knows what he must get rid of if he wants to lay up treasure in heaven, but apparently he feels it is not a good bargain for him. Jesus loves the man and is deeply saddened by his selfish choice.

❑ *Luke 18:35–19:27.* The major events take place in Jericho: the healing and acceptance of discipleship by the blind beggar and the fine reception Zacchaeus gives Jesus in his home. These two events close Luke's so-called "Gospel of the Outcasts," found in Luke 15–19.

The blind beggar near Jericho hears "the crowd going by." When he asks about what is happening, they tell him about Jesus. The beggar immediately calls to Jesus, "Jesus, Son of David"—which is the only time Luke records the use of this phrase in his Gospel. Jesus restores his sight, and the blind beggar who was an outcast becomes a follower of the greatest rabbi ever known.

Zacchaeus becomes a follower too, though he lived on the opposite side of the tracks. Zacchaeus, a chief of lesser tax collectors, sees Jesus from the perspective of the branches of a sycamore-fig tree. He takes up where the rich ruler left off—he gives half of what he owns to the poor and promises to repay much more than the law requires if he has taken money falsely or forcibly. He too becomes a follower and goes to Jerusalem with perhaps 150 or more of Jesus' followers on their way to observe Passover.

❑ *Luke 19:28-44.* Jesus enters Jerusalem to begin his last week of life on earth. He sends two of his disciples to bring a certain colt for him to ride. As the disciples untie the colt, the colt's owner asks, "Why are you untying the colt?" The disciples answer, as Jesus had instructed them, "The Lord needs it."

Jesus enters Jerusalem as a man of peace, not war; humble, not proud; with love, not with "swords loud clashing." Multitudes of followers parade around him, placing their cloaks on the road. The followers cry out,

> Blessed is the king who comes in the name of the Lord!
> Peace in heaven and glory in the highest!

This statement reminds us of the angels' song at Jesus' birth. (See Luke 2:14.)

THE KINGDOM OF GOD

The blind beggar, Zacchaeus, Mary, Martha, Lazarus, Simon the leper, and scores of followers join in Jesus' great demonstration of his messiahship as he fulfills the prophecy of Zechariah 9:9. On Palm Sunday he comes as the triumphant Prince of Peace. As Jesus rides on the colt in majesty, he weeps for David's capital city of Jerusalem; for the people know not "what would bring you peace." Yet embodied in Jesus now, as at his birth in the manger of Bethlehem, unheard voices sing, "Peace in heaven and glory in the highest!" (19:38).

DIMENSION THREE:
WHAT DOES THE BIBLE MEAN TO ME?

The Key to the Kingdom of God

The basic theme running through this lesson is the key to the kingdom of God. The key is made of costly discipleship quickly owned and gladly assumed, conscientious concern that the nature and character of God not be violated but released through us as channels of his Spirit.

The key to the Kingdom is not hard to find; it is not hidden in some dark, dismal place. It is quickly and easily available, for we find it in our hearts—our attitudes, our motives, our dispositions, our yearnings, our commitments. The meaning of the Scriptures for me is the discovery of the key to life, to the abundant life found in Christ about whom simple shepherds heard the heavenly choirs declare, "Peace on earth." Augustus Caesar is not our good news, our God, or our Savior (as the Roman Senate declared him to be). Rather, it is the Babe grown to maturity who willingly asserted the mind of Christ, even when he faced the horrors of the pain-racked cross. Jesus is the only person who ever "imitated" fully the character and lifestyle of God. As Jesus asks his followers to imitate him, so he imitated God. Those who imitate God as seen in Christ embody the Lord's Prayer. They truly bear his name: Christ-ians, Christians! The fruit of prayer as Jesus prayed is to become a child of God—heir of his spiritual treasures: love, justice, kindness, mercy, concern, firmness in doing right, dedication to doing the word of God.

Jesus' statement to Zacchaeus continually challenges us: "Zacchaeus, come down immediately. I must stay at your house today" (19:5). Zacchaeus did not invite Jesus to go home with him; Jesus simply tells Zacchaeus that he is going home with him. What kind of friends would Jesus find at Zacchaeus's?

Suppose you knew Jesus was going to stop over in your house. Would you want to hurry home to put certain magazines and books behind the shelves and display the Bible in a prominent place? Jesus says, Rubbish! He wants to see us in our natural habitat and begin where we are. In fact, Jesus will call every person in the household to become followers.

Heaven and earth will pass away,
but my words will never pass away (21:33).

— 11 —
Jesus Responds to
Difficult Questions
Luke 19:45–21:38

DIMENSION ONE:
WHAT DOES THE BIBLE SAY?

Answer these questions by reading Luke 19:45–20:18

1. Whom does Jesus drive out of the Temple? (19:45)

2. Who seeks to kill Jesus? (19:47)

3. What question do the chief priests, teachers of the law, and elders ask Jesus? (20:2)

4. What question does Jesus ask them? (20:4)

5. In the allegory of the wicked tenants, what do the tenants do to the first servant? (20:10)

6. After sending the third servant to no avail, whom does the owner of the vineyard send? (20:13)

7. What do the tenants do to the beloved son? (20:15)

8. What will the owner of the vineyard do? (20:16)

Answer these questions by reading Luke 20:19–21:4

9. What does Jesus say to those seeking to trap him on the issue of paying taxes to Caesar? (20:24-25)

10. What question do the Sadducees ask Jesus about a woman who married seven brothers? (20:33)

11. Why do the teachers of the law answer, "Well said, teacher!"? (20:39-40)

12. Of whom are the disciples to beware? (20:46)

13. Why does Jesus say the poor widow put more in the treasury "than all the others"? (21:4)

Answer these questions by reading Luke 21:5-38

14. When Jesus tells them that one day the Temple will be destroyed, what do the disciples ask? (21:7)

15. When will be the time for the disciples to be witnesses? (21:12-13)

16. Why do they not need to worry before answering questions? (21:14-15)

17. How will they save their lives? (21:19)

18. When they see Jerusalem surrounded by armies, what has come near? (21:20)

19. What is Jesus' prediction about Jerusalem and her people? (21:24)

20. When the Son of Man returns, where will they see him? (21:27)

21. What will all the physical changes in the earth mean? (21:28)

22. When the trees sprout leaves, what will they know? (21:29-31)

23. What does Jesus say will not pass away? (21:33)

24. What is Jesus doing during the day? (21:37)

DIMENSION TWO:
WHAT DOES THE BIBLE MEAN?

The theme for this session deals with how Jesus responds to difficult questions. The Scripture is divided into three themes:

1. Opposition of the Sanhedrin (19:45–20:18)
2. Three Basic Questions (20:19–21:4)
3. Events That Mark the End of the Age (21:5-38)

❏ *Luke 19:45–20:18.* This lesson resonates with Jesus' anger against the manner in which the priests misused their responsibilities. Jesus had cleansed the Temple; that is, he had defied the chief priests and their high priest (Caiaphas). They were the owners of "The Booths of Annas"—the booths where sacrificial animals were sold to pilgrims who came to Jerusalem to worship. The many ordinary priests were assigned various duties under the leadership of the captain of the Temple (second only in rank and power to the high priest). The chief priests were the wealthy aristocrats of Jerusalem and had tremendous power and authority.

As Jesus watched the sale of unblemished sacrificial animals, such as lambs, bullocks, and pigeons, he witnessed the fruit of greed. Poor pilgrims from foreign lands would come with an animal they valued and would offer it to the priests for inspection for sacrifice. All too often the priests would find a defect, such as a tuft of black wool in among the white wool, and declare the lamb blemished. The priests were only too glad to offer one of the unblemished sheep from their flock—making a large profit. Jesus also watched the moneychangers exchange Roman, Greek, Syrian, and Ethiopian coins for the Temple coins—again making unjust profits from pilgrims who came to worship the Lord. The priests had turned the house of prayer into a den of robbers. In righteous anger Jesus chased the animals out of their stalls and overturned the tables of the moneychangers. No wonder the House of Annas (which currently controlled the business of the Temple) was furious at Jesus—so much so that Caiaphas, with influence from his father-in-law, Annas, called a meeting of the Sanhedrin to decide what to do with Jesus.

Against this background we see the Messiah having to face verbal traps carefully developed by the chief priests, teachers of the law (and Pharisees), and the principal men (elders) of the people—that is, the members of the Sanhedrin.

The first question addressed to Jesus was, "Tell us by what authority you are doing these things?" (20:2). This was a carefully worded question. If Jesus said, "God told me to do these things," they would say he blasphemed God. If Jesus said, "I do these things because my audience wants and needs them," they would say he was a revolutionary and would report to the governor (Pilate) that he was starting a messianic revolt against Rome. Jesus turned the tables by saying, "I will answer your question after you answer one of mine, namely, By what authority did John baptize in the Jordan? Was it from God, or was it a man-devised scheme?" If they said, "By God ("heaven"),

Jesus would say, "Then why didn't you believe him and be baptized by him?" If they said, "John was a skilled dramatist; he had a public relations committee who planned his meeting places and orchestrated the emotions of the crowds," such a statement would cause a riot by hundreds who had felt the presence of God through John. So the Sanhedrin cannot answer Jesus' question—and he does not answer theirs.

Jesus then addresses a parable (in the form of an allegory) to the "committee" from the Sanhedrin. The wicked tenants are obviously the priests (the religious leaders) who have done all they could to thwart God's work through Jesus and who eventually will kill him in their attempt to gain the divine inheritance (the kingdom of God) in their "specialized" way. God (the "owner of the vineyard") sent servants (prophets) three times to his tenants (the religious leaders—teachers of the law and priests) to receive fruit from their vine; but each time the tenants treated his servants very badly, abusing and shaming them. Finally, God (again, the owner of the vineyard) sent his beloved son to the tenants (leaders); but they killed him, hoping to gain the inheritance for themselves through such action (20:9-18).

The response of the people to the allegory was, "May this never be!" But the attitudes of the religious leaders toward Jesus remained the same. Luke then states that Jesus, looking firmly into their faces, said (combining two passages of Scripture [Psalm 118:22 and Isaiah 8:14-15] into one statement), " 'The stone the builders rejected has become the capstone.' Everyone [Jew] who falls on that stone [of messianic faith] will be broken to pieces, but he [who disbelieves] on whom it [the rock of faith] falls will be crushed."

The members of the Sanhedrin "looked for a way to arrest him immediately, because they knew he had spoken this parable against them. But they were afraid of the people."

❑ *Luke 20:20–21:4.* The story continues. The members of the Sanhedrin send spies to watch Jesus, hoping he will say something they can use against him. They ask Jesus, while pretending to be sincere, "Is it right for us to pay taxes to Caesar or not?" Jesus perceives their craftiness and asks them for a coin ("a denarius"). Taking the denarius in hand, he lifts the coin so all can see and asks, "Whose portrait and inscription are on it?" They answer, "Caesar's." "Then give to Caesar what is Caesar's, and to God what is God's." They were not able to catch him by what he said; "and astonished by his answer, they became silent" (20:20-26).

Jesus was a master logician, but more: He faced issues squarely. In this case he affirmed payment of the annual tax by all males over fourteen years of age and also affirmed the need to give to the King of kings what he demanded, a committed life.

Another question raised, this time by the Sadducees who seek to trap Jesus in a Pharisaic doctrine, is the belief in resurrection, life after death (20:27-40). With a grin on his face, a priest asks about a woman who married a man with six brothers. Her husband died without offspring; so his first, then second, brother married her—but no offspring. Finally, all seven brothers had married her. In the hereafter which brother would be her husband? (Certainly not all seven! This would hardly suggest "paradise"—one woman with seven husbands. Surely the crowd laughed.) Jesus points out that the priests do not know their own Scriptures—including the Book of Deuteronomy (25:5-6, which is the basis for the discussion) and Exodus 3. Jesus points out that Yahweh (God) revealed himself to Moses, saying, "I am the God of your father, the God of Abraham . . . Isaac, and . . . Jacob." God is not the God of the dead but the living. So the Pharisees are correct; there is life after death. That is, God is the Lord of living, thinking, responsive beings.

Then Jesus turns to the Pharisees and points out their theological error: When a Jew (who is accounted worthy) dies, his body is dead; but his spirit continues alive and active. Dead persons are like the angels; they are spirit, not matter. Hence they do not face the question as to how many spouses they have in paradise. (See 1 Corinthians 15.) Some teachers of the law (who were also Pharisees) say, "Well said, teacher!"

Jesus' question as to how the Christ (Messiah) could be David's son and at the same time David's Lord (20:41-44) is asked with one purpose in mind. Jesus wants to make clear that his understanding of what God's Messiah is to be is not the same as that of the Davidic dynasty. Jesus is denying verses 42-43 as a valid messianic statement (He refused to be such a coercive Christ at the time of his baptism.). He is a son of David genealogically, but he is not David's kind of "anointed" Christ.

Jesus, as he watches the rich ostentatiously drop their metal coins with a prolonged clatter (indicating quantity) into the treasury receptacles, notes a widow who dropped her last two coins almost silently, because of their small size, into the treasury. Jesus says, "This poor widow has put in more than all the others. All these people gave their gifts out of their wealth; but she out of her poverty put in all she had to live on" (21:3-4). ❑ *Luke 21:5-38.* In summary, Jesus says, (1) Herod's temple will be destroyed [which event took place thirty-five years later]. (2) The prophetic day of the Lord will come as judgment against those engaged in evil (sin against God). (3) Christ will come "in a cloud," even as God's presence was made known through the cloud as Moses met God at the door of the Tent of Meeting. (We must be careful in overemphasizing our metaphors, lest they become the reality itself.) (4) The persecution and martyrdom of faithful Christians is inevitable (as Luke learned when he walked with Paul for thousands of miles to take the gospel to Europe.)

DIMENSION THREE:
WHAT DOES THE BIBLE MEAN TO ME?

Luke 20:41-44—The Son of David

Luke 20:41-44 again raises the question about the identity of Jesus. Now his hearers consider what it means for him to be "the son of David," probably the greatest and most revered of all the kings of Israel. Even so, David had some obvious faults and had committed some magnificent sins. Nevertheless, the Messiah is to be from the lineage of David.

Is Jesus to be a new, improved King David, following not just the genealogy, but the military and political career as well? If so, how does Jesus' three-year career of story-telling, healing, and aggravating the religious and civil authorities fit with the image of the great King David? How can someone who associates so much with the fringes of society, instead of the mighty fighting men of David's armies and the Temple officials, hope to have anyone think he comes after the example of David? How has Jesus turned upside down the expectations and images of who he, and thus, the Messiah is?

We have found this man subverting our nation.
He opposes payment of taxes to Caesar and claims
to be Christ, a king (23:2).

12

Jesus Faces His Disciples and Accusers
Luke 22:1–23:25

DIMENSION ONE:
WHAT DOES THE BIBLE SAY?

Answer these questions by reading Luke 22

1. As the Feast of the Passover draws near, what group of persons plot to get rid of Jesus? (22:2)

2. To whom does Judas go to betray Jesus? (22:4)

3. How do Peter and John know where Jesus and the disciples will observe the Passover meal? (22:10-12)

4. After Jesus gives thanks for the wine, he says he will not drink wine until some great event occurs. What is this great event? (22:18)

5. As they celebrate the Passover, where is Judas? (22:21)

6. How does Jesus deal with the disciples' dispute about who is the greatest among them? (22:26)

7. What does Jesus tell Peter will happen before the rooster crows this day? (22:34)

8. What does Jesus ask of God in his prayer at Gethsemane? (22:42)

9. What does Jesus say when Judas draws near to kiss him? (22:48)

10. What is Jesus' reaction when one of his disciples tries to protect him with a sword? (22:50-51)

11. What does Jesus say to the chief priests, officers of the Temple guard, and elders? (22:52)

12. Where do they take Jesus? (22:54)

13. On what three occasions does Peter deny knowing Jesus?
   (22:56-60)

   1.

   2.

   3.

14. When the rooster crows, who turns and looks at Peter?
   (22:61)

15. What do the men who hold Jesus in custody do to him?
   (22:63-65)

16. When day comes, where does the council of elders take
   Jesus? (22:66)

17. What does the council ask of Jesus, and what is his reply?
   (22:67-69)

18. With one voice they ask, "Are you then the Son of God?"
   What is Jesus' reply? (22:70)

19. Where do the religious leaders take Jesus then? (23:1)

20. What charges do the religious leaders bring to Pilate against Jesus? (23:2)

21. What question does Pilate ask Jesus? What is Jesus' response? (23:3)

22. Learning that Jesus is a Galilean, to whom does Pilate send Jesus? (23:6-7)

23. How do Herod and his soldiers treat Jesus? (23:11-12)

24. Pilate offers to punish and release Jesus. For whose release does the crowd cry? (23:18-19)

DIMENSION TWO:
WHAT DOES THE BIBLE MEAN?

The Scripture for this lesson is divided into four themes:

1. Jesus' Last Supper (22:1-23)
2. Jesus' Last Teachings to His Disciples (22:24-38)
3. Jesus in Gethsemane and His Arrest (22:39-65)
4. Jesus' Condemnation (22:66–23:25)

❏ *Luke 22:1-23.* This section of the lesson is based on the Passion narrative. The Passion narrative in Luke generally refers to Jesus' suffering prior to the cross, beginning with his arrest in Gethsemane. The Passion narrative also includes the Feast of the Passover and the Last Supper.

The Passover begins at 6:00 P.M. in the evening of the fourteenth day of the month of Nisan (Exodus 12:18; Deuteronomy 16:1-8). For the Jews, a new day begins at sunset. The Feast of the Passover celebrates the night that the people of Israel, through a special act of God, won their freedom from oppressive slavery under the Egyptian pharaoh. God saved all the first-born among the Israelite males through an act of faith: After slaughtering a lamb, a bunch of hyssop dipped in the blood of the lamb was dabbed on the lintel and two doorposts of each house occupied by an Israelite. When the angel of death came, the Lord would "pass over" the marked doors. In the future, when children ask what this festival service means, the parents are to say, "It is the Passover sacrifice to the LORD" (Exodus 12:26-27).

Jesus wants to observe this Passover with his disciples. At this time, the chief priests and scribes of the Sanhedrin seek ways to put Jesus to death (22:2).

Luke 22:7-13 describes how Jesus plans for the Feast of the Passover. The disciples will know the place for the feast by looking for a man carrying a pitcher of water. They are to follow him and enter the house he enters. Inside the home, they are to tell the householder, "The Teacher asks: Where is the guest room, where I may eat the Passover with my disciples?" The disciples find the man, he shows them the room, and they prepare the meal.

When the hour comes, that is at sunset, they sit down. Matthew 26:21 and Mark 14:18 record knowledge of Judas's future betrayal as they eat. In Luke, Jesus mentions his betrayal after they have eaten the bread and drunk the wine. (See 22:21-22.) Jesus takes a cup; and after he gives thanks to God, he says, "Take this and divide it among you."

❏ *Luke 22:24-38.* Luke purposely places verses 21-30 here in order to compare two types of unworthy thinking. One disciple (Judas) is thinking of informing the priests as to where they might find Jesus and thus arrest him. Perhaps Jesus will take the militant posture of King David's offspring. The other disciples involve themselves in a dispute as to who is to be regarded as the greatest. Comparing Judas's breach of faith with the other disciples' desire for a position higher than the others—well, none of them comes through with flying moral colors!

Jesus interprets greatness in the kingdom of God as the reverse of what the "world" wants. The person who serves is greater than the one who sits at table!

As Jesus thinks about the disciples' personal goals of achieving greatness, he must feel tremendous pain, knowing they will not stand by him in his hour of greatest need. Each and all will forsake him, even Simon Peter. (See 22:31-34.) Why do followers of Jesus think of greatness in the kingdom of God in materialistic terms? Those who are great in the kingdom of God measure achievements in nonphysical terms, such as truth, honesty, purity, justice, kindness, loyalty, and love.

Luke 22:39-65. At this point Jesus leaves the upper room and goes to the Mount of Olives. Luke does not name the garden of Gethsemane or Golgotha.

Arriving at the Mount of Olives, Jesus struggles in prayer with the consequence of his calling. Jesus is in agony, and his sweat becomes like great drops of blood. Through prayer he commits himself to the fulfillment of his mission as the Messiah of God. He will be loyal to the lifestyle God has called him to fulfill. He moves from weak surrender to strong assertion of the will of God. He will bear witness as God's Messiah even unto death.

Before dawn, his disciples hear the noise of the approaching Temple guards. Judas comes to greet Jesus with a kiss; but Jesus stops him by saying, "Judas, are you betraying the Son of Man with a kiss?" (22:47-48). The guards arrest Jesus and lead him to the palace of Caiaphas.

❏ **Luke 22:66–23:25.** Many of the religious leaders gather at the chief priest's palace for a predawn meeting. They abuse Jesus in many ways (22:63-65). The need for haste is evident; that evening at 6:00 P.M. all Jews want to celebrate the sabbath. No criminal can be left alive on a Roman cross after sunset. So, in the next eleven hours, Jesus must be tried, crucified, and killed. No wonder that as soon as the Council convenes, they order Jesus to speak: "If you are the Christ . . . tell us." Jesus then uncooperatively responds, "If I tell you, you will not believe me, and if I asked you, you would not answer. But from now on, the Son of Man will be seated at the right hand of the mighty God." Immediately they demand, "Are you then the Son of God?" Jesus responds, "You are right in saying I am" (which in Aramaic means yes).

Various trials move quickly. Audience is granted by Pilate. Speakers for the Sanhedrin charge Jesus with sedition and acts of perversion (23:2). Pilate, the procurator of Judah, asks Jesus, "Are you the king of the Jews?" Jesus' reply is an Aramaic idiom: "Yes, it is as you say," which means yes.

But the "yes" is a partial response. I believe that what Jesus would love to have done is to finish the sentence: Yes, I am the king of the Jews—in the sense of being the King (Messiah) of the kingdom of God. No, I am not a king in a political sense. I have no army, no palace, no weapons, no throne. I am God's Messiah.

"But they insisted, 'He stirs up the people all over Judea by his teaching. He started in Galilee and has come all the way here.' " The word *Galilee* works like magic. Pilate sends Jesus to Herod Antipas, in whose tetrarchy Jesus is a citizen. Let Antipas pass judgment! (See 23:6-7.) Herod has wanted to see Jesus for a long time (23:8). But Jesus says nothing in his presence. "Then Herod and the soldiers ridiculed and mocked him. Dressing him in an elegant robe, they sent him back to Pilate" (23:11).

The sequence of trials, in a matter of three or four hours, is unbelievable. Finally, Pilate, as was his custom at Passover, offers to set one prisoner, Jesus, free. But the crowd demands, "Away with this man! Release Barabbas ["son of a rabbi," a murdering insurrectionist] to us!" The crowd demands freedom for the murderer and crucifixion for Jesus. So Pilate lets their voices prevail.

DIMENSION THREE:
WHAT DOES THE BIBLE MEAN TO ME?

Luke 22:1-6, 47-53—Will You Betray Me?

At the Mount of Olives, the disciples have fallen asleep. Jesus rouses them with a rebuke, but his words are cut short by the arrival of Judas. Judas arrives with an armed crowd to arrest Jesus. The bitterness of betrayal is indicated by the attempted kiss of a trusted friend. Judas's action is an example of denying Jesus. And Peter, who is so certain that he will not fall away, denies Jesus three times. Peter rejects Jesus' call to follow in suffering. Peter has chosen safety over discipleship. He has broken his relationship to Jesus.

The Gospel of Luke urges us to understand the reason for the disciples' failure. Evidently, Luke wishes to show that denial of Jesus is a sign of failure.

Is it possible that we misjudge the seriousness of our failings as disciples in a similar way? Discuss possible indications of this misjudgment.

Father, into your hands I commit my spirit (23:46).

— 13 —

Jesus Experiences Calvary and Resurrection

Luke 23:26–24:53

DIMENSION ONE: WHAT DOES THE BIBLE SAY?

Answer these questions by reading Luke 23:25-56

1. Who carries Jesus' cross behind him? (23:26)

2. What do the women who were in the large number of people who followed Jesus do? (23:27)

3. What does Jesus say to them? (23:28)

4. Why does Jesus say this? (23:29)

5. How many other persons are led away with Jesus to be put to death? (23:32)

6. Where do they take the three men? (23:33)

7. After they crucify the three men, what does Jesus say? (23:34)

8. Following Jesus' prayer, what do they do? (23:34b)

9. Who sneers at, mocks, and insults Jesus and what does each say? (23:35-39)

10. Who defends Jesus? (23:40-41)

11. What is Jesus' response to the man's request to remember him when "you come into your kingdom"? (23:42-43)

12. From the sixth until the ninth hours, what two major events take place? (23:44-45)

13. What are Jesus' last words on the cross? (23:46)

14. When the centurion sees what has taken place, he praises God. What does the centurion say about this event? (23:47)

15. What do the various people do at Jesus' death? (23:48-49)

16. Who asks Pilate for Jesus' body? (23:50-52)

17. What do the women who have come with Jesus from Galilee do that afternoon? (23:54-56)

Answer these questions by reading Luke 24

18. What do the women discover when they reach the tomb? (24:2-3)

19. What were the women wondering about, and who appears to them? (24:4-5)

20. What do the two men ask the women to remember? (24:6-7)

21. As two disciples walk toward Emmaus, who joins them? (24:13-15)

22. After Cleopas and his companion summarize what has taken place in Jerusalem during the past three days, what does Jesus say? (24:25-26)

23. What opens the eyes of Cleopas and his companion to Jesus' identity? (24:30-31)

24. What happens when Cleopas and his companion tell the Eleven and those who are with them about their experience? (24:36)

DIMENSION TWO:
WHAT DOES THE BIBLE MEAN?

The Scripture for this lesson is divided into four themes:

1. From the Cross to the Burial (23:25-56)
2. Discovery of the Empty Tomb (24:1-12)
3. Jesus' Appearance After Resurrection (24:13-43)
4. Christ's Parting From His Disciples (24:44-53)

❏ *Luke 23:26-56.* The last lesson mentioned how Herod and the soldiers mocked Jesus. When Pilate finally ordered that Jesus be crucified, soldiers led him to "the place called the Skull." (In Latin, "the Skull" is translated "Calvary"; in Aramaic [Jesus' language], it is translated "Golgotha.") It got its name either because the place resembled a skull or because many skulls were left there from other crucifixions.

106   LUKE

As the soldiers lead the three men to their horrible fate, they realize Jesus is unable to carry his cross beam. He has been abused severely for hours. They compel a pilgrim to the Passover, Simon of the city of Cyrene in North Africa, to carry the cross of one who would become his Lord.

The "daughters of Jerusalem" who weep for Jesus (but apparently not for the criminals) may have heard him teach and perhaps felt his power in their lives. He tells them not to weep for him, but for their children; for Jerusalem's future is bleak.

They nail Jesus' hands to the cross beam, lash it to a pole, and drop the cross into a hole. The cross drops with a thud, bringing an unbelievable surge of pain. In terrible agony Jesus prays, not for himself, but for his executioners and probably even for the religious leaders who coerced Pilate to put him on the cross: "Father, forgive them, for they do not know what they are doing" (23:34). Roman custom permitted the executioners to take a criminal's clothes and divide them among themselves as they willed. They cast lots to divide his clothes (see Psalm 22:18), and "the people stood watching" (23:35).

Three different groups scoff at, rail against, and mock Jesus. All the religious leaders were required by law to be present in Jerusalem for the Feast of the Passover. Probably many chief priests, "ordinary priests," and Levites join the "rulers" of the Sanhedrin as they shout, "He saved others; let him save himself if he is the Christ of God, the Chosen One."

A second group is the soldiers. The third group includes the two criminals, one of whom witnesses the way Jesus responds to hate and torture of body and mind and, as a result, concludes that Jesus cannot have done wrong. This criminal turns his face to Jesus and says, between agonizing moments of cramping muscles and searing fire in hands and feet, "Jesus, remember me when you come into your kingdom." Jesus senses the respect and honor of this suffering man in the tone of his voice and replies, "Today you will be with me in paradise" (23:43). What amazing grace!

From noon until three, "darkness came over the whole land . . . for the sun stopped shining" (23:44-45). During this three-hour period, as Matthew (27:46) and Mark (15:34) state, Jesus cries out, "My God, my God, why have you forsaken me?" (See Psalm 22:1.)

At the end of six hours of unbelievable torment (physical, mental, and spiritual), Jesus dies, with the prayer his mother taught him as a little boy on his lips and in his heart: "Father, into your hands I commit my spirit" (23:46).

Mary, his mother, would feel a sword pierce her soul as she remembered her sweet baby boy saying his prayers; and now he prays for the last time. Perhaps John, into whose care Jesus has given his mother, looks at her and nods knowingly (John 19:25-27).

A centurion (in charge of one hundred soldiers) exclaims, "Surely this was a righteous man" (23:47). Spectators at the Crucifixion go home frightened and "beat their breasts" in repentance, while the followers of Jesus are stunned and stand "at a distance, watching these things" (23:48-49).

Two groups make burial arrangements. Joseph of Arimathea took the body down from the cross, wrapped it in linen, and put the body in a tomb. The women of Galilee who came with Jesus on his mission to Jerusalem "saw the tomb and how his body was laid in it. Then they went home and prepared spices and perfumes" (23:55-56) for embalming his body—which they never use, for his body is not in the tomb when they arrive Sunday morning.

❏ *Luke 24:1-12.* When the women from Galilee arrive at the tomb, two men ask them, "Why do you look for the living among the dead?" (24:5). Obviously, Jesus is alive.

If you were to witness to an unbeliever about Jesus—about what happened between Friday at 3:00 P.M. and Sunday at 6:00 A.M.—what would you say? I believe God raised Jesus from the dead at Joseph's tomb. Also, Jesus has a different body, just as real as a physical body, but a spiritual body—unhampered by time and space. His presence can clearly be known, to which witness we now turn.

❏ *Luke 24:13-43.* On Sunday morning, Cleopas and his companion (wife?) are on the way to Emmaus, about seven miles from Jerusalem. As they walk, they discuss the amazing and frightening experiences of the past three days. As they talk, a stranger joins them. Before long, he is explaining the past events (which involved the trial, crucifixion, and burial of Jesus) in terms of biblical passages. Soon their hearts burned within them, strangely warmed at the realization of truth put so simply that it could not be missed.

Cleopas and his companion invite the stranger to stay for a meal. As the guest thanks God and breaks bread, he becomes known: Jesus. They immediately return to Jerusalem and share their experience with the Eleven and those who are with them. They are greeted with the news that Jesus has also appeared to Simon. Thus they accept the truth about Jesus and can say, "It is true! The Lord has risen" (24:34). Take time to discuss how Cleopas and his companion recognized Jesus that day. Luke states that Jesus "took bread, gave thanks, broke it and began to give it to them" (24:30). The disciples recognize him, and then he disappears—without eating bread.

Luke 24:36-43 creates a problem. It states that Jesus eats broiled fish and can be touched physically. The question is this: Was Jesus in the Spirit or in a physical body? The early Christians faced a theological heresy, called docetism, that claimed Jesus did not have a physical body. Therefore he never needed to eat or sleep, never experienced cold weather or pain, even at the Crucifixion—he was entirely and always pure spirit, spirit only!

The content of Luke 24:36-49 tries to deal with such heresy, showing that Jesus is "real." Many persons assumed that being "real" meant to be physical. Yet most affirmed that after the death of the physical body, Jesus was raised, as Paul says, "a spiritual body" (1 Corinthians 15:44). The risen Lord does not need physical food to sustain his spiritual body—he is free of it; he is parted from it; he is ascended from such a material limitation. Resurrection sets him free. He has moved from a perishable body to an imperishable body.

While Cleopas and his companion were telling the Eleven and the others about their encounter with the risen Lord, "Jesus himself stood among them" (24:36). Being in Jesus' presence is a great, but frightening, experience. Many of us have had similar experiences with the risen Christ.

❏ *Luke 24:44-53.* Luke briefly describes Jesus' parting "ascension" from his disciples as he blessed them. (You may want to note Luke's second reference to the Ascension in Acts 1:1-11.)

DIMENSION THREE:
WHAT DOES THE BIBLE MEAN TO ME?

Luke 24:36-43—Physical Body or Spiritual Body?

We noted the difficulty in interpreting Luke 24:36-43. Let us examine the implications of Paul's view in 1 Corinthians 15:42-44. Paul states clearly and emphatically that we all have a physical body here on earth. At death, we *change* to another form. At death, the physical body of a Christian changes into a different form. We are structurally different; we become a spiritual body.

One way to understand this dilemma of Luke 24:36-43 is to recall Luke's explanation (1:1-4) of how he obtained information to write his Gospel. He talked to many types of people whose experiences inevitably differed. This passage represents one of Luke's sources. Notice that each Gospel writer rejected some data. For example, one story tells how Jesus when he was a boy played with a neighbor friend, Xeno. One time while playing tag on the flat roof of Xeno's house, Jesus sidestepped and Xeno fell to the ground. He screamed as he fell. Xeno's mother came out of her house and accused Jesus of murdering her son. To deal with this difficult situation, Jesus went to the body and said, "Xeno, rise from the dead. Didst I kill thee or not?" Xeno opened his eyes and said, "No, my Lord, Thou didst not kill me. Thou didst resurrect me from the dead."

Luke did well not to include this kind of illustration of Jesus' boyhood days. It does not help us understand the boy Jesus, nor does Luke 24:36-43 help us deal with the issue of the spiritual body of Jesus after the Resurrection. Perhaps Luke should have omitted this passage from his Gospel, too. (What do you think or feel?) How can we find consistency (freedom from contradiction) between Paul and Luke on this question? Is consistency necessary?

As in Jesus' experience, the physical body is not the same as the spiritual body. They are "two in one." Death does not conquer the real person, Jesus. At death, his physical body dies; three days later, at Resurrection, his whole being (body and spirit) changes into a spiritual body. At death, Christians are freed from the bonds of the physical, with no limitations of time or space and with an at-one-ment with God.